55
50¢

D1195990

This book may be kept

Research Studies in Library Science, No. 14

RESEARCH STUDIES IN LIBRARY SCIENCE
Bohdan S. Wynar, Editor

Weeding
Library Collections

Stanley J. Slote

Department of Library Science
Queens College
City University of New York

1975

Southern Baptist College
FELIX GOODSON
LIBRARY
Walnut Ridge, Ark.

Libraries Unlimited, Inc., Littleton, Colo.

Copyright © 1975 Stanley J. Slote
All Rights Reserved
Printed in the United States of America

LIBRARIES UNLIMITED, INC.
P.O. Box 263
Littleton, Colorado 80120

Library of Congress Cataloging in Publication Data

Slote, Stanley J
    Weeding library collections.

    (Research studies in library science ; no. 14)
    Bibliography: p.
    Includes index.
    1.   Discarding of books, periodicals, etc.
I. Title. II. Series.
Z703.6.S55   025.2'1   74-23062
ISBN 0-87287-105-3

42,548

O25.21
S256w

ACKNOWLEDGMENTS

Special thanks must be given to the following people who assisted the original research projects: Professors Ralph Blasingame, Thomas Mott, Ernest R. DeProspo, Neal Harlow, Joseph Naus, and Philip Clark. In addition I was assisted in my field work by James E. Bryant, William Urban, Veronica Carey, Marian Gerhardt, Bettie Diver, Audrey Tirendi, and Barbara Hull.

Much assistance was received from Mary F. Tomaselli, Carol L. Ginsburg, Ronnie E. Teich, Juliette Levinton, Miriam Guido, and Salvatore M. Addotta, who edited the entire manuscript and helped put it into its final form.

Mary F. Tomaselli is author of the index.

TABLE OF CONTENTS

APPENDICES

LIST OF ILLUSTRATIONS

PREFACE

This book is based upon two recent research projects in weeding and identifying core collections. However, it became apparent that the principles and techniques studied are applicable to almost all types of library collections.

This work has been designed to be used for four distinct purposes:

1. As a comprehensive source summarizing the opinion, knowledge, and serious research in the field of weeding. The author's own research is reported in such detail that replication of the studies is possible. In addition, this book contains the first report of the Harrison Study.

2. As a do-it-yourself guide for librarians wishing to weed out their present collections. It is the aim of this book not only to explain and justify its methods, but to include a step-by-step procedure for "weeding without tears."

3. As a textbook in library schools, especially in courses that deal with the acquisition and maintenance of library collections, for weeding is one of the best techniques available for the long-range building of useful collections.

4. As a stimulus to further study in this entire area. It is hoped that libraries using the recommended methods will measure and report upon the costs of weeding and the impact of such weeding upon changes in the amount of circulation and in user satisfaction.

The two parts of the collection that can be identified with confidence are the "core collection" (which will satisfy 95 percent to 99 percent of the demands upon the present collection) and a "weedable" part (which represents very little use-potential—1 percent to 5 percent). It might be helpful to think in terms of "positive selection" (the volumes to be retained in the core) and "negative selection" (the volumes to be weeded). Thus, the term "weeded" is used as an antonym for "core collection."

It is not suggested that the "weedable" part of the collection be destroyed, thrown out, or even removed from the library. There is sympathy, but not agreement, with Carter Davidson, who suggested that libraries "burn, bury, sell or give away the rest [i.e., the weeded collection]."[1] No judgment is made other than to identify this part of the collection as having little practical use. The author is not out to destroy society's literary heritage. On the contrary, he feels strongly that ideally *any* book should be made readily available to *everyone*, as *rapidly* and *painlessly* as possible. Thus, secondary storage, centralized regional collections, and other subordinate means of preservation are implied. Nevertheless, the author feels strongly that the weeded volumes should be segregated and removed from the open stacks or primary areas which house the regular circulating collection.

While this book is based partially upon a doctoral dissertation, to which frequent reference will be made (the *Five Library Study*), an attempt has been made to exclude the more obscure and complex aspects of the original dissertation. Some of the details of the dissertation have been retained in the appendices of the present work, for the sake of the more research-oriented readers. Readers interested in the statistical evidence and the detailed methodology of the original project are advised to read the original work.[2] Nevertheless, the conclusions of the present work have been based upon controlled study, statistical verification, and several field studies. Its concepts have been applied and verified.

The study of the serious literature in weeding is an essential part of this report. The literature tended to validate the author's findings and to indicate the applicability of the methods and techniques to other types of collections, especially university and college collections. It is for this reason that the more serious works are covered in some detail.

Stanley J. Slote
November 14, 1974

REFERENCES

1. Carter Davidson, "The Future of the College Library," *College and Research Libraries* IV (March 1943), pp. 115-16.

2. Stanley James Slote, "The Predictive Value of Past-Use Patterns of Adult Fiction in Public Libraries for Identifying Core Collections" (unpublished Ph.D. dissertation, Rutgers University, 1970). University Microfilms, Inc., Ann Arbor, Michigan, No. 71-3104.

"What are countless books to me,
and libraries of which the owner
in his whole life will scarcely read
the titles?"

—Seneca

Part 1

Background and Introduction to Weeding

CHAPTER 1

BACKGROUND TO WEEDING

INTRODUCTION

It has long been an expressed standard of libraries to weed collections on a regular basis. For instance, the *Proposed Standards for Adult Services in Public Libraries in New York State*, 1969, states:

Withdrawal

Much of the material in the community library is expendable within ten years.[1]

Annual withdrawals ... should average at least five percent of the total collection.[2]

These typical statements are only two of dozens of such statements that can be found; they consistently recommend the removal of books from the collection. Even more specific advice can be found in the ALA pamphlet, *Weeding the Small Library Collection*.[3] Here a six-page detailed paper has been issued to encourage library weeding. It is a "why, when, who, and how" pamphlet which advises librarians to "take courage and weed." In addition, leading practitioners of librarianship have called for continuous and aggressive weeding of collections. Carter and Bonk call for weeding to be a "regular, continuing, and steady process."[4] McGaw says that it improves the "efficiency and vitality of a collection."[5] Anderson points out that unnecessary items weaken a library.[6] Over the years librarians have been barraged by an almost endless stream of advice of this sort.

In spite of the advice, however, it has been observed and reported that too little weeding is being practiced and that library shelves contain quantities of unused and unwanted materials. It is hard to find a practicing librarian who feels that sufficient weeding is being done in his library.

REASONS FOR WEEDING

In the face of rapidly growing collections, shortage of space and the high cost of storing books on open stacks, there are rather potent reasons for vigorous weeding. It has been reported that Yale can store "four and one-half times as many books . . . by the Yale Compact Storage Plan as in conventional stack arrangement."[7] This use of compact storage for less-used materials should not be overlooked, especially in the face of growing resistance to budget increases for new construction now being experienced in *all* types of libraries.

It should be noted that an increase in stack space is often the immediate cause of a much larger construction program. The real impact of expanding collections beyond their present library capacity must be related to the proper balance and functioning of the entire library. If one assumes that in the designing of new libraries an idealized relationship between book and non-book space is achieved, then the addition of new books beyond the original capacity of a building has some very expensive implications. In 1973, *Library Journal* reported that 143 new public library buildings had an average cost of $38.28 per square foot, or about $10.94 per volume of designed book capacity.[8] On an average the architects designed new buildings to contain 3½ volumes per square foot of enclosed floor area. The $10.94 in capital costs per volume to build a proper new library does not include the cost of land, furniture, and many other indirect expenses. Therefore, libraries considering the expansion of their collections could well consider this additional cost as the probable long-range result of such expansion.

Two related aspects of these costs might be considered. In 1973, for instance, the costs of building new academic and public libraries ranged from $3 per volume capacity to $55 per volume.[9] This seems to indicate that a wide range of factors are involved, and that a new library may find itself spending considerably more or less than $10.94 per volume for expansion. This observation calls for more study and analysis, with the goal of creating greater efficiency in the design of new facilities. However, the $10.94 figure must be considered only a point of departure when one considers the cost of expansion.

The other aspect, rarely mentioned in the literature, is that the actual space taken up by books is such a small part of a new library building. Fremont Rider mentioned that only 10 percent of the cubic area taken up by book stacks contains books.[10] In 1972-73, *Library Journal* reported that academic libraries were built having a book capacity between 1½ and 6½ volumes per square foot of enclosed space.[11] This means that at full capacity a library actually used about 1/40th, or 2½ percent, of its enclosed area for books.[12] Thus it seems reasonable, when thinking of expanding collections, to think in terms of the true needs: on an average every book added over the designed capacity of a library should ultimately require building expansion equal to forty times the amount of space taken up by the actual book itself.

While compact storage is less expensive than open stack storage, other suggestions to solve the over-all space problem should not be overlooked. One of the most obvious is to substitute some type of microfilm for the usual hard-covered book. Unfortunately, until greater user acceptance is gained, it is likely that such a solution would reduce usage considerably and at the same time increase service costs.

FACTORS DISCOURAGING WEEDING

In view of the pressing space problems it is difficult to understand why more weeding has not been undertaken. A number of factors have discouraged weeding.

Emphasis on numbers. The number of books in a library is often considered a criterion of the quality of a library. Thus librarians, playing the numbers game, may tend to keep obsolete books to be included in the official book count. While many librarians reject the validity of a number count as a sensible quality measure, the official reporting forms for years emphasized book counts in the data to be submitted to higher authorities.

Professional work-pressures. Weeding has generally been considered a professional task. In many instances work-pressures have not left librarians much time to perform the tasks of weeding. When it is considered that not only must weeding decisions be made, but that the card catalog, shelf list, and other records be maintained, the tasks and the time required to do them became intimidating to understaffed libraries.

Sacredness of collection. There are emotional and intellectual blocks against removing books from a collection. Many people consider books to be valuable records of human heritage and therefore almost sacred. The removal of any book becomes painful. Such indiscriminate retention of books does not serve the public. Books that are not being used but that have historical value belong in a depository. A public library that is *serving* the public needs to have a collection that is up to date and changing.

Collections will change, however, in spite of efforts to keep them intact. What is available to the reader is *not* what has been so carefully selected and purchased. Access to the reader is reduced by:

1. Theft and vandalism. Collections do not consist of all the books which have been purchased. Losses due to theft and vandalism will change a collection. Collections are routinely weeded of the newest and most wanted volumes, by the patrons themselves. Thus the original collection, which was carefully selected, is not the collection that remains on the library's shelves.

2. Misshelved books. A misshelved book generally no longer exists for the reader. He is unlikely to have access to it either through the card catalog or through normal browsing in subject areas—two basic access points to a collection. Unless shelf-reading is constant, regular, and careful, a part of the collection has disappeared (for all practical purposes) just as surely as if the books had been stolen. Furthermore, especially in academic libraries, intentional misshelving is a common technique that a patron uses to assure temporary but easy access to a particular book. If this practice is not prevented, the working collection is considerably different from the collection originally acquired.

3. Circulation. Circulating collections are not intact since substantial segments are in the hands of the clients. It is not uncommon to have a fourth of a collection circulating at any given time. Of the volumes that are circulating most will eventually be returned, but there are a certain number of books which, by virtue of being much wanted, will almost always be out. Faculty loans in college and university libraries often are non-recallable and therefore not part of the readily usable collection. As far as the user is concerned, he is not dealing with the collection as originally established, but with a collection that is on the shelves at the moment he is in the library. Therefore, it is inconsistent to maintain that the collection acquired is identical to the collection available. An attack on weeding cannot be based on the concept of keeping the integrity, unity, and overall design of the collection. Such unity has already been destroyed.

Conflicting criteria. Hard-to-apply and sometimes conflicting criteria have often made weeding an arduous and disturbing task. Weeders are torn between keeping the books people want and the "good" books. Librarians want balance, wide subject coverage, and quality. An attempt was made to apply these criteria when the volumes originally were selected. Then the weeder, frequently the person who selected the book in the first place, must make a subjective decision to discard a book previously judged worthy. This makes for difficult decision-making.

The weeding process is not without its risks. How many librarians are there who wished they had saved old telephone directories, mail-order catalogs, local newspapers, and a wide range of other items now sought after? Katz points out that the vast majority of nineteenth century local newspapers were completely destroyed, with, at best, only given issues saved.[13] As anyone who has ever cleaned out an attic or basement knows, only a few days pass before a use is found for something just irretrievably discarded. In libraries this risk must be minimized by some centralized responsibility for the collection of less-used materials.

While this study is unable to overcome the resistance caused by all of the above factors, it has aimed at making the physical and intellectual processes of weeding much simpler. If *objective* weeding criteria are used, weeding decisions are easier to make. Even clerical personnel, presumably more available than professionals, can be utilized for this work. With more certainty in weeding decisions, more extensive weeding could be done.

SUMMARY

It seems extremely timely that more attention be focused on weeding. Librarians are faced with economic pressures and demands for accountability for their expenditures. If ever there were a time for innovation in library services, attitudes, and operations, it is now. If, by realistic thinning of collections, librarians can reduce their requests for increased capital costs and at the same time increase the services being rendered, they will be answering the challenge in a way most acceptable to society.

REFERENCES

1. New York Library Association, Standards Committee and Sub-committees of the Adult Services Section, *Proposed Standards for Adult Services in Public Libraries in New York State* (New York: Library Association, March 1969), p. 7.

2. Ibid., p. 8.

3. American Library Association, Small Libraries Project, *Weeding the Small Library Collection.* Supplement A to Small Libraries Project Pamphlet No. 5 (Chicago: American Library Association, 1962).

4. Mary Duncan Carter and Wallace John Bonk, *Building Library Collections* (3d ed.; Metuchen, N.J.: Scarecrow Press, 1969), p. 138.

5. Howard F. McGaw, "Policies and Practices in Discarding," *Library Trends* IV (January 1956), p. 277.

6. Polly G. Anderson, "First Aids for the Ailing Adult Book Collection," *Bookmark* XXI (November 1961), p. 47.

7. Lee Ash, *Yale's Selective Book Retirement Program* (Hamden, Conn.: Archon Books, 1963), p. 52.

8. Hoyt Galvin and Barbara Asbury, "Public Library Building in 1973," *Library Journal* XCVIII (December 1, 1973), p. 3517.

9. *Library Journal* XCVIII (December 1, 1973), pp. 3511-23.

10. Fremont Rider, *Compact Book Storage* (New York: Hadham Press, 1949), p. 8.

11. Jerrold Orne, "Academic Library Building in 1973," *Library Journal* XCVIII (December 1, 1973), pp. 3511-16.

12. The computation for arriving at this figure uses 6 x 9 in. as the size of the average volume, a figure reported by Kilpatrick and Van Hoesen as the size of the median volume in their study, "The Heights of Three Hundred and Fifty Thousand Volumes," which appeared in the July 1935 issue of *Library Quarterly*. By sampling a number of volumes, we estimate the average width of a volume to be 1-2/3 in. This means that the average volume contains 90 cubic inches. Figuring the average library to have 8 foot ceilings, and therefore 8 cubic feet of volume per square foot of floor space, and using the 3½ books per square foot as reported above, we find that the average new library has 7/16th of a book (or 41 cubic inches) per cubic foot of enclosed area. This works out to about 2½ percent of the 1728 cubic inches in a cubic foot.

13. William A. Katz, *Introduction to Reference Work, Vol. II: Reference Services* (New York: McGraw-Hill, 1969), p. 87.

CHAPTER 2

TRADITIONAL APPROACHES TO WEEDING

CONVENTIONAL GUIDELINES TO WEEDING

While many authorities have recommended weeding, it should be emphasized that opinions on weeding have not been unanimous. Some have suggested either no weeding or weeding with great limitations. In addition, even those recommending it have stated a diversity of goals for this activity. Much of this diversity of opinion reflects the philosophies, concepts, attitudes, and prejudices of the writers. More often, the opinions are the results of practical problems facing administrators of ever growing collections. The concept follows the need. Finally, there have been opinions based upon the needs of specific research projects, where assumptions are forced upon a researcher if his studies are to have some broad-based foundation. All these influences can be seen in the following goals:

That all collections should be kept absolutely intact. Books represent the accumulated recorded written heritage of civilization; therefore, wherever they may be, they should be preserved. This is the position of the anti-weeder. The removal of anything is considered profane. Typical of this attitude is an article by John Neufeld, entitled "S-O-B Save Our Books." The term "s.o.b." pretty much sums up his reaction toward anyone attempting to remove any book from a collection.[1]

That collections may be weeded, gingerly, by professionals only, using good judgment, not rules. Only the experienced and trained librarian can perform this task. However, general guidelines for weeding can be established. The goal is to maintain a well-balanced collection that will match the needs and the wants of users, real and potential. Libraries attached to other institutions (schools, universities, or businesses) should have a further review of the books recommended for weeding, to be performed by members of the main institution (teachers, professors, researchers). Otherwise, "good" books or "useful" ones are likely to be removed.

This position probably represents the majority opinion in the country today. It has been reinforced by unpleasant experiences when weeding has been handled by non-librarians. It has been generated by the alienation of members of faculties, for example, when weeding has occurred without their being consulted. In part, this position has been taught in library schools and represents an honest belief of some of the leaders in the profession. Typical of this attitude

8

is that of Bedsole who insists that "sound professional judgment of any specific work will always be required."[2]

Even people who have strongly suggested other methods, which they have validated by rigidly disciplined research, are hesitant to offend professionalism. Fussler, who has done some of the most fruitful investigation in the field of weeding, felt forced to defend himself in the face of rather severe criticism from the faculty:

> Furthermore there is little question that the overall effectiveness of any formula for selecting books for storage [weeding] would be improved considerably if one or more scholars reviewed the titles recommended for storage.[3]

This conclusion is *not* supported by any research evidence in his studies, and in fact might be in direct *conflict* with his findings.

That collections should be so weeded that they are maintained at a predetermined physical size. This aim, popular with some administrators, is an attempt to relieve the pressure for new construction caused by the ever growing collections.

This approach is taken by Silver in a term paper prepared for an operations research course at the Massachusetts Institute of Technology (M.I.T.):

> One serious problem now confronting the librarians is that the extra shelf space is rapidly diminishing due to the acquisition of new books. A possible course of action to remedy the situation is the use of weeding.[4]

Silver feels that it would be useful to librarians to find a way to keep constant the number of volumes in a collection.

This approach, as with all the others, is not without its critics. Rider implies that such stabilization of the size of a collection is not feasible. He maintains that as human knowledge grows, so must libraries. Just in one area, reference, the number of books gets larger each year. No college has succeeded in stabilizing collections. The continuations of periodicals, government documents, society transactions, etc., prevent stabilization.[5]

That library stacks should be stocked with those volumes likely to give the library the greatest circulation. This objective highlights the need for getting maximum usage out of social institutions and their resources. It also points up the conflict between two schools of librarianship: those who wish to give the user what he *wants*; and those who wish to give him what he *needs* (or what is "good" for him).

NEWER GUIDELINES TO WEEDING

That weeding should increase circulation. One must search thoroughly in order to find support for weeding to maximize use; it sounds unprofessional and therefore is best approached more indirectly. Gans states that "a library that is not used sufficiently is a waste of resources, ... the library must be user-oriented."[6] More to the point is a study by Ruth Polson. She reports an 81 percent increase in circulation, "despite a decrease of more than one-third in the book stock," after weeding. The tone of her report implies that weeding is a tool for circulation increase.[7]

That collections should be weeded so that the speed of access is increased and so that the accuracy in retrieval is improved. It has been observed, mainly in special libraries, that small compact collections of materials reduce the time needed for retrieval.[8] In libraries where speed is essential, this is often a prime consideration. For instance, in newspaper libraries (morgues) where deadlines must be met, the growth of collections and cumulation of irrelevant materials can block reasonable usage.

That those books least likely to be used in the future be removed. In contrast with the goals of maintaining collections at a given size, this approach attempts to keep a collection that will satisfy a predetermined amount of future use. It tries to identify core collections that will satisfy 95 percent or 99 percent of the present demands made upon the collection, and to do this with the smallest identifiable core collection. A very large part of the serious research in weeding has used this approach. As Fussler and Simon state:

> The major purpose of the study was to answer this question: Will any kind of statistical procedure predict with reasonable accuracy the frequencies with which groups of books with defined characteristics are likely to be used in a research library?[9]

One characteristic of these studies is the implication that weeded books be removed to secondary storage in less accessible areas. Another recurring theme relates to the endless growth of the size of collections and the constant pressure for new buildings. The studies often attempt to determine long-range solutions and frequently try to make predictions of the percentages of the collection that can be removed at various levels of retained usage. They accept, as a basic premise, that usage is a valid criterion for keeping volumes on open stacks, or in main library buildings. Furthermore, they aim to find objective criteria for weeding. This present volume has accepted these assumptions as being basic to its theme.

ADDITIONAL METHODS

While all of the above reflect some current goals of weeding, other methods of reaching these same goals have been suggested. It is obvious, for instance, that the space needed to store materials can be reduced substantially through the use of micro-reproduction. Microfilm, microfiche, and microprint can be found in libraries. While many people feel that such reduction in size makes the materials harder to use, the whole question of size reduction is an important but unresolved one.

In addition, libraries have attacked the problems through limiting the subject areas of their collections or assigning different specializations to other libraries in a cooperative fashion. The Library of Congress has agreed with the National Library of Medicine and the Department of Agriculture Library not to overlap their specialized collections unnecessarily. The Farmington Plan, now defunct, was another attempt to assign areas of subject or language specialization.

Many other attempts have been made. Union catalogs, interlibrary loans, deposit collections, and library systems have all contributed in some way toward fulfilling the above goals.

REFERENCES

1. John Neufeld, "S-O-B Save Our Books," *RQ* VI (Fall 1966), pp. 25-28.

2. Danny T. Bedsole, "Formulating a Weeding Policy for Books in a Special Library," *Special Libraries* XLIX (May-June 1958), p. 207.

3. Herman H. Fussler and Julian L. Simon, *Patterns in the Use of Books in Large Research Libraries* (Chicago: University of Chicago Press, 1969), p. 144.

4. Edward A. Silver, "A Quantitative Appraisal of the M.I.T. Science Library Mezzanine with an Application to the Problem of Limited Shelf Space" (unpublished term paper for M.I.T. graduate course 8:75, Operations Research, 1962), p. 2.

5. Fremont Rider, *The Scholar and the Future of the Research Library* (New York: Hadham Press, 1944), pp. 44-46.

6. Herbert J. Gans, "The Public Library in Perspective," in *The Public Library and the City*, ed. by Ralph W. Conant (Cambridge, Mass.: M.I.T. Press, 1965), p. 69.

7. Ruth E. Polson, "When Your Library Joins a System, What Can You Expect?" *Illinois Libraries* XLIX (January 1967), pp. 26-38.

8. Stanley J. Slote, "An Approach to Weeding Criteria for Newspaper Libraries," *American Documentation* XIX (April 1968), p. 168.

9. Fussler and Simon, *Patterns in the Use of Books in Large Research Libraries*, p. 5.

SOUTHERN BAPTIST COLLEGE LIBRARY

CHAPTER 3

LIBRARY STANDARDS RELATING TO WEEDING

A study of the various standards will show that weeding is either recommended or completely disregarded; it is never suggested that no weeding be done. If recommended, however, the force with which weeding is emphasized varies considerably. These standards range from 1) no weeding, to 2) minimal weeding, to 3) rather forthright statements quantifying the process. Listed in this chapter are some examples of standards in the order of their emphasis. No attempt has been made to be all-inclusive. Accreditation standards, state and local standards, and standards found in textbooks have been omitted. The statements below are generally national standards formulated or accepted by a national library or an educational or governmental organization.

In general, the types of standards relating to weeding may be divided into five classifications.

STANDARDS NOT MENTIONING WEEDING

The 1969 *Standards for School Media Programs*[1] and *Guidelines for Establishing Junior College Libraries*, 1963[2] make no mention of weeding at all. These standards generally are concerned with promoting the establishment or recognition of relatively new kinds of libraries. Apparently, it is hard to think in terms of weeding a library which has not yet come into existence, or which has only recently been established.

STANDARDS THAT HINT AT WEEDING

Some standards just hint at a need for weeding. The *Standards for Children's Services in Public Libraries*, for example, handle weeding almost parenthetically:

Continuous critical evaluation of children's materials throughout the development of the collection—in initial selection, replacement, duplication, and *withdrawal* [italics mine]—is essential to maintain the effectiveness and quality of resources.[3]

Even less forceful is the approach found in *Objectives and Standards for Special Libraries*. Here the writer tries to report what actually is happening in practice, rather than what should happen.

THE SIZE OF A SPECIAL LIBRARY COLLECTION DEPENDS UPON THE AMOUNT OF MATERIAL AVAILABLE THAT IS PERTINENT TO THE ORGANIZATION'S SPECIAL NEEDS.

The purpose and use of the special library's collection influence its size. Some libraries need large reference collections, multiple copies, and works that have historical value; others have highly selective collections, keep currently useful literature only, and retain only in microform older periodical sets and items of decreasing usefulness. *Many libraries discard little used materials if they are available in the area.* [Italics mine.] The rate and direction of growth of the library's collection should reflect the continuing requirements of the library's clientele.[4]

Another approach focuses on replacement: discarding is recommended only when new editions are acquired. *Recommended Standards for Libraries in Hospitals* uses this approach:

Out-of-date editions must be replaced by the most recent as soon as possible, and discarded from stock. An outdated book is a trap for the unwary student.[5]

STANDARDS RECOMMENDING WEEDING

The third case of standards specifically recommends weeding, occasionally identifies what is to be weeded, but does not tell how often, how much, or even how. For example, the *Standards for Library Services in Health Care Institutions* says:

Regular replacement of worn-out and outdated library materials should be planned and budgeted annually.[6]

Selection of materials should be based on an established written policy. . . . This policy should cover scope of subject matter, retention periods, acceptance of gifts, and criteria for weeding and discarding.[7]

Somewhat more specific, but still rather limited, are the standards in the ALA *Standards for College Libraries*:

Obsolete materials, such as outmoded books, superseded editions, incomplete sets of longer works, broken files of unindexed journals, superfluous duplicates, and worn out or badly marked volumes, should be continuously weeded, with the advice of faculty members concerned.[8]

In line with this type of recommendation are the following three Standards published in 1964 by the Department of Health, Education and Welfare:

> 1. *Recommended Standards for Junior High School Libraries*
> The collection should be kept up-to-date and in good condition by continuous discarding, binding, and addition of new titles.[9]
>
> 2. *Recommended Standards for Senior High School Libraries*
> Provision should be made through an adequate budget for the continuous process of replacement of out-of-date titles with new editions, of worn copies with fresh ones, of obsolete titles with current ones.
> There should be regular replacement of encyclopedias by the purchase of one new set of the latest edition every other year. . . .[10]

In this last recommendation there is the first glimmer of specific instruction in the specifics of weeding:

> 3. *Recommended Standards for Junior College Libraries*
> This standard calls for "systematic and regular discarding of obsolete materials."[11]

Young Adult Services in the Public Library provides more emphatic recommendation of weeding, but weeding criteria are vague:

> The young adult collection should be drastically weeded to keep it alive, fresh, and attractive. Titles that are not read with interest should be discarded. Care, however, should be taken not to discard unusual and special titles which need to be introduced by the librarian to the young adult to show their true values. In the field of sports, vocational titles, and junior novels, where there is a plethora of titles, it is advisable to limit rebinding and replacement to the most useful and outstanding books, and to use available funds to purchase new titles to round out the collection.[12]

The older *School Library Standards*, now superseded by *Standards for School Media Programs*, also recommends weeding in general terms:

> The collections are continuously re-evaluated in relation to changing curriculum content, new instructional methods, and current needs of teachers and students. Appropriate materials are obtained for these new developments. This process of re-evaluation

also leads to the replacement of outmoded materials with those that are up-to-date, the discarding of materials no longer useful, and the replacement of materials in poor repair.[13]

It is assumed that certain factors tend to operate to keep sufficient balance between materials acquired and those discarded, so that the materials collections, particularly in very large schools, do not become disproportionately large.[14]

This latter assumption is rather questionable when compared to the observable facts.

STANDARDS ESTABLISHING QUANTITIES

The fourth class of standards not only specifically requires weeding, but makes some attempt to establish weeding criteria and to define the amount of weeding that is advisable. *Public Library Service* (1956) not only explains that currently *useful* books are dead after 10 years but advises a reduction in the collection at the average rate of 5 percent through weeding:

Systematic removal from collections of materials no longer useful is essential to maintaining the purposes and quality of resources.

Unnecessary items remaining in a collection can weaken a library as surely as insufficient acquisitions. In time such material characterizes the whole collection, over-shadowing newer and more useful purchases. Outdated material should obviously be removed; discredited material deserves the same action, although this requires more judgment; and items no longer of interest should give way in the process so appropriately termed "weeding." With few exceptions, public libraries are not centers for historical research, except in the field of local history when not adequately supplied elsewhere in the community. They do not need to retain material for a possible future scholar, and their day-to-day effectiveness for regular users decreases as they keep seldom-used material. The currently useful books which form the bulk of material in a public library collection are expendable or "dead" within ten years.

Annual withdrawals from the collection should average at least 5 percent of the total collection.[15]

In 1962, the *Interim Standards for Small Public Libraries* accepted most of the above standards, some of them verbatim; but the *Interim Standards* highlighted the need for preserving some of the weeded material in larger centers:

SYSTEMATIC REMOVAL FROM THE LIBRARY OF MATERIALS NO LONGER USEFUL IS ESSENTIAL TO MAINTAIN THE PURPOSE AND QUALITY OF THE COLLECTION.

1. Outdated and shabby material should obviously be removed; discredited material deserves the same action, although this requires more judgment; and items no longer of interest should be weeded out.

2. Material not actively used in small libraries but still occasionally needed should be withdrawn from the collection and sent to an authorized library center from which it can be borrowed for future use.

3. Annual withdrawals from the basic collection should average 5 percent of the total collection. In community libraries where much of the material is in a changing collection, this percentage may be lower.[16]

In 1967, the *Minimum Standards for Public Library Systems* again retained verbatim substantial sections of both the 1956 and 1962 standards but expanded upon them. While both quantitative and qualitative, they inject a note of uncertainty that has characterized weeding efforts in libraries. The entire section is quoted since it is interesting to note the specific word changes and to speculate on the attitudes that may have caused such changes. (Basic changes in content have been italicized.)

SYSTEMATIC REMOVAL OF MATERIALS NO LONGER USE-FUL IS ESSENTIAL TO MAINTAINING THE PURPOSES AND QUALITY OF *RESOURCES*

Outdated, *seldom-used*, or shabby *items* remaining in the collection can weaken a library as surely as insufficient acquisitions. In time such material characterizes the whole collection, over-shadowing newer and more useful purchases. Outdated materials should obviously be removed. With few exceptions, community libraries are not centers for historical research, except in the field of local history. Except for materials of special quality smaller community libraries do not ordinarily need to retain seldom-used items, for to do so may decrease day-to-day effectiveness. Larger community libraries whose *staff and building are adequate for proper maintenance of a more varied collection* may be more generous in retention of seldom-used items.

i. Annual withdrawals from community library collections should average at least 5 percent of the total collection. The community library collection should consist of currently useful materials. The bulk of material in the smaller community library is expendable or "dead" within ten years.

ii. Headquarters libraries, reservoirs of quality materials from which community libraries draw, should carefully consider withdrawals and not necessarily make them conform to numerical ratios.

iii. *Withdrawals made at any level should be offered to the next higher echelon of resources before they are destroyed.*[17]

It can be seen from the changes that three new emphases have been made. First, there is a focus on seldom-used materials. Such a use-criteria for weeding can lead to a realistic solution of weeding problems. Second, the offering of resources to higher echelons centers on the need to have different depths for different kinds of collections. Finally, the need for a larger staff for proper collection maintenance is also highlighted. However, in these standards adequate staff justifies less weeding, while for most practicing librarians it would permit more weeding.

Another quantified example is mentioned in the now superseded *Standards for School Library Programs*:

Back issues of periodicals needed for reference work and for other purposes are retained in the school library for a time span covering at least five years.[18]

Note, however, that this approach tells how long an item is to be kept at a minimum and not when it is to be discarded.

RECOMMENDED STANDARDS

The author recommends a fifth version of standards for libraries. This would be a standard, including all of the following points, for material that normally circulates.

1. The objective of weeding would be to maintain a core collection of books that would satisfy 95 percent to 99 percent of the present demands made upon the entire present collection.

2. All books weeded would be considered for secondary or centralized storage.

3. One complete weeding of the library should take place in each year.

4. The weeding criterion to be used should be based solely upon the likelihood of a volume's being used in the future.

5. The shelf-time period established for each library should satisfy the above standards and should result in an objective similar to this: "All volumes should be removed that have not been circulated since (date)." This shelf-time period should take into account the use patterns of no less than one full year.

6. Similar criteria should be established and utilized, in modified form, for the different *types* of material as follows:

a) For runs of periodicals, remove all before a specific publication date. This date should be established separately for each run.
b) For reference books, weeding should be performed as for circulating works, attempting to keep a core representing 99 percent to 99.5 percent of the present usage.
c) For archives and special works (such as works of local authors) no weeding should be done.

The basis for such standards will be developed in later chapters of this work. No such official standards exist at this time. However, some individual libraries are using the above standards, at least in part.

REFERENCES

1. American Association of School Librarians and the Department of Audiovisual Instruction of the National Education Association, *Standards for School Media Programs* (Chicago: American Library Association, 1969).

2. American Library Association, Association of College and Research Libraries, Committee on Standards, "Guidelines for Establishing Junior College Libraries," *College and Research Libraries* XXIV (November 1963), pp. 501-505.

3. American Library Association, Public Library Association, Subcommittee on Standards for Children's Service, *Standards for Children's Services in Public Libraries* (Chicago: American Library Association, 1964), p. 22.

4. Special Libraries Association, "Objectives and Standards for Special Libraries," *Special Libraries* LV (December 1964), p. 675.

5. Library Association, Hospital Libraries, *Recommended Standards for Libraries in Hospitals* (London: Library Association, 1965), p. 15.

6. American Library Association, Association of Hospital and Institution Libraries, *Standards for Library Services in Health Care Institutions* (Chicago: American Library Association, 1970), p. 13.

7. Ibid., p. 8.

8. American Library Association, Association of College and Research Libraries, Committee on Standards, "Standards for College Libraries," *College and Research Libraries* XX (July 1959), p. 277.

9. U.S., Department of Health, Education, and Welfare, *Survey of School Library Standards*, by Richard L. Darling, Circular No. 740, OE 15048 (Washington, D.C.: Government Printing Office, 1964), p. 42.

10. Ibid., p. 45.

11. Ibid., p. 48.

12. American Library Association, Public Library Association, Committee on Standards for Work with Young Adults in Public Libraries, *Young Adult Services in the Public Library* (Chicago: American Library Association, 1960), p. 27.

13. American Library Association, Association of School Librarians, *Standards for School Library Programs* (Chicago: American Library Association, 1960), p. 75.

14. Ibid., pp. 82-83.

15. American Library Association, Public Libraries Division, Co-ordinating Committee on Revision of Public Library Standards, Public Library Service, *A Guide to Evaluation, with Minimum Standards* (Chicago: American Library Association, 1956), pp. 34-35.

16. American Library Association, Public Library Association, Sub-committee on Standards for Small Libraries, *Interim Standards for Small Public Libraries: Guidelines Toward Achieving the Goals of Public Library Service* (Chicago: American Library Association, 1963), p. 8.

17. American Library Association, Public Library Association, Standards Committee and Subcommittees, *Minimum Standards for Public Library Systems, 1966* (Chicago: American Library Association, 1967), pp. 39-40.

18. American Library Association, Association of School Librarians, *Standards for School Library Programs*, p. 79.

CHAPTER 4

PRESENT WEEDING CRITERIA
BASED ON JUDGMENT

DIFFICULTIES ENCOUNTERED IN
SUBJECTIVE WEEDING

The mass of material. In the face of rather indecisive standards or goals for the weeding of libraries, there exists a wide range of specific advice on what to weed. Much of this advice assumes that librarians have the ability to make "good" weeding judgments, based upon their knowledge of the community, of the users, of books in general, of their own collections, and of society's needs.

It is the contention of this writer that the above assumptions lack the validity usually assigned to them. For example, librarians are supposed to "know" books: to know what exists, what is worth acquiring, what the library holds, and what the library should hold. Can anyone really "know" about books? It is doubtful. The very mass of the accumulation seems to make it improbable. It is likely that there are between 35,000,000 and 40,000,000 different titles or works in the world.[1] The holdings of just a few of the major libraries seem to point to the validity of the estimate, although no definitive study has been made on the titles now in existence. Nevertheless, the British Museum contains 7,000,000 volumes of which 75 percent are not among the 13,500,000 books held by the Library of Congress. Bibliothèque Nationale, with a strong emphasis on French works, contains 7,000,000 volumes. To this quantity, one must also consider the 400,000 new titles added internationally each year. In addition, the several hundred thousand government documents (restricted and unrestricted) published each year are generally not included in the 400,000 figure. To make the problem more complex, one might want to include the 1,000,000 serial titles, current and retrospective, and hundreds of thousands of other non-book items such as newspapers, phonograph records, pamphlets, films, film strips, and other forms collected by some libraries. The size of the stockpile creates an awesome problem for the librarian.

One of the ways librarians obtain information about books is through critical reviews. Unfortunately, only a small fraction of books published are reviewed. And even the reviews that do exist are a massive body of literature.

Another way to "know" books is to read them. A reasonably fast reader, with enough time (our average librarian?), might read one book a day. This would amount to 365 books per year or one-thousandth of the current output and perhaps one-hundred thousandth of the total of all works that exist. This does not even begin to deal with other serious problems that block this approach, such as one reader's inability to handle the diversity of languages, or the lack of availability of these volumes to librarians.

Can a librarian really "know" books? It is hard to believe that such knowledge can be anything but extremely perfunctory. It is hard even to "know" the literature in one restricted field like librarianship. There are at least 700 periodicals of librarianship. Counting regional periodicals, irregular ones, and newsletter types, the number must exceed 1,000. How many of these does the average librarian get to read? It is difficult to find anyone, even in the academic world, who feels that he keeps up with the literature of librarianship.

Knowledge of the community. Other assumptions upon which subjective weeding is based also have serious flaws. For example, librarians are charged with "knowing their communities" and thereby "catering to their needs." Is this possible? How many people even know their own needs and can cater to them? Or the needs and wants of their children? Their students? What unique characteristics, training, and experience do librarians have that equips them for such a commitment? If it is true that they understand and know how to serve their communities, why have they not done it?

Every survey of use shows that libraries get relatively little use. It has been estimated that only 10 percent of the adult population really uses the public library[2] and that a large percentage of college students use their college library so rarely "that they would scarcely miss it if it ceased to exist."[3] Librarians have trouble satisfying the needs of their patrons, much less the community.

Consider the frequent failures that occur when the library tries to serve minority groups and the poor. No matter how exhaustive a study of a community is, there exists no agreed upon, specific, or valid response to the data. Do Spanish books substantially increase library usage by Puerto Ricans in New York? Do black studies and black subjects fill libraries with black readers? The answer to both questions, at least to now, is a qualified "no."

Therefore, the author tends to reject the purely professional and subjective approach to weeding. The assumption that librarians really "know" what books to retain to satisfy the patron is invalid, unless it is based upon *use studies* within a library. Furthermore, attempting to keep what is best for some vague non-user seems a waste, considering the difficulties encountered in trying to satisfy completely the present users. Why look for new challenges before responding to the older, closer, and more immediate challenge of running present libraries better?

In reading the following weeding criteria one must be suspicious of the basis of the judgments which created them. Nonetheless, these criteria do create a starting point for current weeding practice.

pp 22-26

Titles

SPECIFIC WEEDING CRITERIA

The following weeding criteria have been culled from the sources in the special bibliography at the end of this chapter. Essentially this information has been published in the how-to literature of librarianship, usually for specific types of libraries. However, where the overlapping is great, no attempt has been made to identify the type of library involved. It is the purpose of this chapter to demonstrate the range of criteria available.

begin here → **Weeding based upon appearance.** The most universally accepted criterion for weeding is based upon the *appearance* of a volume. Often, however, this criterion calls for caution—to avoid discarding rare books—and for judgment—to determine whether or not the volume should be replaced. Some of the specific advice is to weed:

1. Books of antiquated appearance which might discourage use.
2. Badly bound volumes with soft pulpy paper and/or shoddy binding.
3. Badly printed works, including those with small print, dull or faded print, cramped margins, poor illustrations, paper that is translucent so that the print shows through.
4. Worn-out volumes whose pages are dirty, brittle, or yellow, with missing pages, frayed binding, broken backs, or dingy or dirty covers.

Weeding of superfluous or duplicate volumes. It is easier for most librarians to agree upon the criterion of weeding duplicate volumes than upon any other criterion since this approach retains one copy of the title in the collection. Books similar to other books fall easily into this category. Some examples to weed are:

1. Unneeded duplicate titles.
2. Duplicates except for date or place or reprint.
3. Inexpensive reprints.
4. Older editions.
5. Editions in languages other than English when the English version is held by the library.
6. Highly specialized books when the library holds more extensive or more up-to-date volumes on the same subject.
7. Superfluous books on subjects of little interest to the local community.

Weeding based upon poor content. Weed:

1. When information is dated.
2. When book is poorly written.
3. When information is incorrect.
4. When improved editions exist.
5. Earlier titles in repetitious fiction series.

Weeding based upon language. Weed:

1. When the language is not called for in your library.

2. Editions in uncommon or foreign languages when edition is also held by library in the native language.

Weeding based upon age alone. Frequently this advice is hedged by exception. Weed:

1. Books held thirty years or less.
2. Books over twenty years old.
3. If not in a standard list and over ten years old.
4. Fiction best sellers of ephemeral value after ten years.
5. Out-of-date books and pamphlets.
6. Books over five years old.
7. Early volumes of serials.

Specific classes of books that particularly lend themselves to weeding. Weed:

1. Books that should not have been bought in the first place.
2. History books with inaccurate or unfair interpretations.
3. Grammars that are old.
4. Ordinary school dictionaries.
5. Almanacs and yearbooks that have been superseded.
6. Religion and philosophy: historical and explanatory texts when superseded; old theology; old commentaries on the Bible; sectarian literature; sermons; books on the conduct of life; popular self-help psychology.
7. In university collections:
    a) Inspirational literature, juveniles, elementary and secondary textbooks, non-contemporary minor authors, crank literature, biographies of obscure people.
    b) Personal war experiences.
    c) Student course outlines.
    d) Correspondence school material.
    e) Accession lists of general libraries.
    f) Press releases.
    g) Publications of colleges and universities: newspapers, newsletters, press releases, humor magazines, literature magazines edited by students; files of programs; non-current books of views, alumni publications.
    h) Programs of meetings.
    i) Speeches of officers of corporations published for purposes of advertising.
    j) Speeches of government officials.
    k) Dissertations.
    l) Subjects of little interest to a specific university because of its curriculum.
    m) Reprints.
    n) Mysteries.

Specific classes of works with specific age for weeding. Weed:

1. All ordinary textbooks after ten years.
2. Medicine, inventions, radio, television, gardening, and business between five and ten years old.
3. Travel books after ten years.
4. Economics, science, and useful arts books in teachers' colleges, when the books are more than ten years old.
5. Fiction best sellers of ephemeral value after ten years.
6. Senior encyclopedias from five to ten years.
7. Encyclopedias at least every ten years.
8. Encyclopedias at least every five years, preferably every year.
9. Junior encyclopedias from three to five years.
10. Almanacs, yearbooks and manuals—get the latest editions, and keep older editions at least five, preferably ten years.
11. Dictionaries—never.
12. Biographical sources—never.
13. Directories after five to ten years but get the latest edition.
14. Inexpensive geographic sources—five to ten years. Expensive ones, never.
15. Social science, topical material, after ten or fifteen years.

Weeding criteria for periodicals and serials. Weed:

1. Periodicals not indexed.
2. Serials that have ceased publication and that have no cumulative index.
3. Incomplete sets.
4. Early volumes of serials, especially longer runs of fifty or sixty volumes.
5. Journals in English petroleum libraries after thirteen years.

An example of specialized weeding criteria (a morgue or newspaper library). These criteria relate to cuts, which are engraved blocks used in the process of reproducing pictures in a newspaper.

1. Discard all cuts of women where the cuts are over ten years old, and any cuts with out-of-date hairdos.
2. Discard all cuts of men, if middle-aged when picture was taken, where the cuts are over fifteen years old.
3. Discard all cuts of men, if under thirty years old when pictures were taken, where the cuts are over ten years old.
4. Discard mats when cuts exist.
5. Keep one good cut of ordinary people.
6. Keep three good cuts of better known people.
7. Keep five good cuts of the famous.
8. Discard bad, blurry, useless cuts.
9. Discard duplicates.
10. Discard all cuts of school athletes five years after they stop playing except those of great national stars. Keep them until death of star.

11. Discard cuts of all professional athletes seven years after they stop playing, except those of big stars. Keep them until death of star.

12. Discard all cuts of the dead, except the famous. Keep these indefinitely.

13. Do not keep wedding, engagement, graduation cuts.

Hundreds of such sets of weeding criteria exist in the area of special librarianship, and this example (produced some years ago by this author) is typical of judgment weeding criteria.

Or again **Weeding criteria based upon use patterns.** While this entire book relates to weeding criteria based upon previous use patterns, the suggested patterns are to be developed by carefully controlled statistical data. The use patterns below were developed as were the other criteria in this chapter—by the judgment of experts. This is what accounts for the wide divergence of opinions. Weed:

1. Books not circulated in three years.

2. Books unused for five years that do not appear in a standard book list.

3. Books that have not circulated for three to five years, that have not been used for reference, and that are not standard titles.

4. If five years old and not circulated in the last year.

5. Books that have not been read in years.

6. Books not called for in a university library in twenty years.

Divergent opinion. It must be emphasized that there is a body of divergent opinion in the area of use patterns.

1. The fact that the volumes are not used in one, two, or five years is not proof that they are not needed.

2. The fact that a book has not circulated during the past few years should not be held to its discredit to an appreciable degree, since potential circulation value may still exist.

3. Discard one-column cuts in their ninth years, unless they have been re-used during this period, in which case they are to be weeded out in the fourteenth year.

Keeping criteria. A word might be added about "keeping" criteria, which are the other side of the coin of weeding criteria. If we know what to keep we can weed the rest. Three examples of this kind of advice follow.

1. Keep if listed in one of the standard catalogs, such as *Standard Catalog for Public Libraries.*

2. Keep if charged out within the past five years.

3. If a title has been frequently used during the past few years, it should probably be retained.

SUMMARY OF WEEDING CRITERIA

Several characteristics of the above criteria might be noted.

1. In many cases, considerable work is needed to apply the criteria. The decision data may be impossible to reconstruct. For example, if the transaction card system is used, how does one tell when or how many times a volume has circulated? Or in another case, the checking of works against a standard catalog is a rather tedious job.

2. In many cases the judgments to be made are based on vague difficult interpretations. What is an "older edition," "small print," "superfluous books on a subject," etc.?

3. There are many contradictions among the criteria.

4. There is, nevertheless, some rationale to much of what is proposed. Many of these criteria seem to satisfy the needs for weeding criteria and might relate closely to more objective criteria produced by careful study.

REFERENCES

1. These figures represent an estimation by the author derived from information obtained from the Library of Congress.

2. Bernard Berelson, *The Library's Public* (New York: Columbia University Press, 1949), p. 10.

3. Harvie Branscomb, *Teaching with Books, A Study of College Libraries* (Chicago: Association of American Colleges and American Library Association, 1940), p. 39.

SPECIAL BIBLIOGRAPHY

The weeding criteria in this chapter are quoted from the following sources:

American Library Association. Small Libraries Project. *Weeding the Small Library Collection.* (Supplement A to Small Libraries Project Pamphlet No. 5.) Chicago: American Library Association, 1962.

Amderson, Polly G. "First Aids for the Ailing Adult Book Collection," *Bookmark* XXI (November 1961), pp. 47-49.

Ash, Lee. *Yale's Selective Book Retirement Program.* Hamden, Conn.: Archon Books, 1963.

Bedsole, Danny T. "Formulating a Weeding Policy for Books in a Special Library," *Special Libraries* XLIX (May-June 1958), pp. 205-209.

Boyer, Calvin J., and Nancy L. Eaton. *Book Selection Policies in American Libraries: An Anthology of Policies from College, Public and School Libraries.* Austin, Tex.: Armadillo Press, 1971.

Branscomb, Harvie. *Teaching with Books, A Study of College Libraries.* Chicago: Association of American Colleges and American Library Association, 1940.

Carter, Mary Duncan, and Wallace John Bonk. *Building Library Collections.* 3d ed. Metuchen, N.J.: Scarecrow Press, 1969.

Cole, P. F. "Journal Usage Versus Age of Journal," *Journal of Documentation* XIX (March 1963), pp. 1-11.

Currie, Dorothy H. *How to Organize a Children's Library.* Dobbs Ferry, N.Y.: Oceana Publications, 1965.

Eliot, Charles W. "The Division of a Library Into Books in Use, and Books Not in Use, with Different Storage Methods for the Two Classes of Books," *Library Journal* XXVII (July 1902), pp. 51-56.

Katz, William A. *Introduction to Reference Work, Vol. II: Reference Services.* New York: McGraw-Hill, 1969.

McGaw, Howard F. "Policies and Practices in Discarding," *Library Trends* IV (January 1956), pp. 269-82.

Mumford, L. Quincy. "Weeding Practices Vary," *Library Journal* LXXI (June 15, 1946), pp. 895-98.

Slote, Stanley J. "An Approach to Weeding Criteria for Newspaper Libraries," *American Documentation* XIX (April 1968), pp. 168-72.

Woods, Donald A. "Weeding the Library Should Be Continuous," *Library Journal* LXXVI (August 1951), pp. 1193-96.

U.S. Department of Health, Education, and Welfare. *Survey of School Library Standards,* by Richard L. Darling. Circular No. 740. OE 15048. Washington, D.C.: Government Printing Office, 1964.

CHAPTER 5

RECOMMENDED WEEDING OBJECTIVES

INTRODUCTION

It seems evident that the objectives of weeding should help fulfill the basic objectives of the library. Libraries claim to have specific, clear-cut goals, but in practice they are likely to have vague, generalized objectives. These objectives, rarely stated clearly or considered in day-to-day decision making, still seem to be in the minds of those administrators running libraries.

Depending upon the library, these objectives might include: supporting school, college, or university curriculum; supporting research efforts in university or special libraries; supplying recreational, informational, and educational services and materials in public libraries; supporting the aims of some larger institutions, as in the case of special libraries; or serving as centers or repositories of civilization's heritage, as with national and major regional libraries. In no case does weeding seem to reduce the ability to fulfill these objectives to any substantial degree. On the contrary, weeding seems to increase accessibility, improve efficiency, reduce costs, and in many other ways improve collections and services to the average user. Even though libraries have goals that vary considerably, they all might gain by using the same general weeding objectives, which could be varied quantitatively depending upon the needs of the clientele.

GOALS RELATING TO WEEDING

It is suggested that the following goals relating to weeding should be considered by libraries:

The primary collection areas are to consist of a core collection of books (and other materials) most likely to be used by the clients. ("Primary collection areas" refers to the open stacks, areas accessible to users, or the other library areas housing the readily available collections.)

The remainder of the books, least likely to be used (the non-core collection) are to be located in secondary storage areas, removed to other libraries, or discarded, depending upon the major objectives of the library and the potential value of the non-core collection. ("Secondary storage areas" refers to compact storage, depository storage, or areas that are less accessible than the primary areas and that represent less expensive storage space.)

The core collection is to retain ____% of the likely future use of the present collection. (The percentage is to be filled in individually for each library depending upon its objectives and the possible unfavorable impact of lost usage upon the clients.) If conditions warrant, the core collection may be broken down into sub-collections by types of material, location, department, service, or in any other convenient way. For example:

1. Reference is to retain ____% of its anticipated future use.
2. The fiction collection ____%.
3. Adult non-fiction ____%.
4. Art is to retain ____%.
5. The Dewey 900's are to retain ____%.
6. Microfilm is to retain ____%.
7. Periodicals are to retain ____%.
8. Branch libraries are to retain ____%.

PROBLEMS RELATING TO THESE OBJECTIVES

In order to implement the above objectives, two immediate problems must be solved.

First, how are the percentages of anticipated future use of a collection to be determined? That question will be answered rather precisely in future chapters. At this point it should be assumed that these percentages can be determined both accurately and practically.

The second problem cannot be dealt with so easily. What percentage of the future usage of a collection should one hope to retain with the core collection? This question entails both personal judgment and practical considerations. Conservative judgments are called for.

An arbitrary figure must be selected. A small public library does not risk much if it retains 95 percent of the anticipated future circulation of the present fiction collection; in fact, even 90 percent might be reasonable.

However, as the data develop, certain practical considerations may assist in making such decisions. In Table 1, from the *Five Library Study* made by this author in 1969, 96 percent of the anticipated future use of the Briarcliff fiction can be retained with 56 percent of the present fiction collection. Ninety-nine percent can be retained with 84 percent of the collection. If the library is pressed for space, and if the additional gain of shelf space is more important than the possible 3 percent loss in usage of this material, then perhaps 96 percent would be a reasonable retention figure. However, if weeding out 16 percent of the collection will solve the current space problem, perhaps it would be better judgment to retain 99 percent of the future use. Of this problem, more will be said later.

Table 1

SHELF-TIME PERIODS OF THE CIRCULATION AND COLLECTION
SAMPLES COMPARED (%)

Cumulative Shelf-Time Period (Mos.)	Briarcliff		Tarrytown		Morristown		Trenton		Newark	
	Circula-tion	Collec-tion	Circula-tion	Collec-tion	Circula-tion	Collec-tion	Circula-tion	Collec-tion	Circula-tion	Collec-tion
0	72	22	69	24	87	41	55	12	49	14
1	79	30	77	34	93	52	65	16	62	19
2	85	37	83	42	97	56	70	20	70	22
3	86	41	85	47	-	60	76	22	75	26
4	90	47	88	51	98	63	79	24	78	29
5	94	52	89	55	-	65	80	27	81	32
6	96	56	91	58	-	68	82	29	83	34
7	97	64	93	61	99	71	85	31	84	36
8	-	68	-	62	-	72	86	33	-	39
9	98	70	94	65	-	74	-	35	87	41
10	-	72	97	67	100	75	88	37	88	42
20	99	84	98	82	-	84	93	53	95	60
30	100	92	-	89	-	90	-	61	97	70
40	-	96	99	94	-	93	97	67	99	74
50	-	99	-	96	-	96	-	72	-	78
60	-	-	100	97	-	-	98	74	-	83
100	-	100	-	99	-	97	99	80	100	92
200	-	-	-	-	-	-	-	92	-	98
300	-	-	-	100	-	100	100	97	-	-
400	-	-	-	-	-	-	-	99	-	100
600	-	-	-	-	-	-	-	100	-	-

SUB-OBJECTIVES RELATING TO THE
MECHANICS OF MEASURING MEANINGFUL
SHELF-TIME PERIODS

In order to assist the entire weeding process, a series of sub-objectives have been recommended. The additional objectives aim: to build in practical safeguards against discarding needed materials; to create meaningful data; and to develop reports about weeding experience that would be useful to others.

In this book, the basic criterion involved in making decisions for keeping or weeding is called "shelf-time period." This period estimates or measures the length of time a book remains on the shelf between successive uses. The author has found, as a result of the studies to be discussed in Part 2, that this criterion is the best predictor of use of a book. The following objectives should be used selectively by individual libraries, depending upon their individual needs, wants, resources, and long- or short-term goals.

That records or controls be established, so that shelf-time periods can be identified. This may be done by any method that would indicate and record circulation and in-library use of library materials.

Mechanically, it can be done by using and keeping intact the circulation records developed when using the book-card method of circulation control; by the use of coded circulation-indicating dots on the back of the book card when using the transaction system for circulation; or by circulation date print-outs for computer circulation systems.

There are several other methods that may be used. The current move toward the transaction card system of circulation control, often with no easily available indication of an individual book's circulation activity, needs to be modified or augmented so that such information becomes available.

Records for non-circulating materials (reference works, reserved collections, bound periodicals, etc.) must be kept if such materials are to be weeded using shelf-time period. This often requires new techniques, records, or procedures.

That procedures and techniques be established that would simplify the compilation of shelf-time period data for individual volumes or materials. For example, when book cards are filled up and there is no space to indicate a new date due, they are frequently removed and replaced with new cards. This destroys the use data. Such old cards should be left in the book, or the last date of use should be transcribed from the old card onto the new card.

A second example would be the application of a coded mark on the spine showing use. Then use data could be observed without removing a book from the shelves.

That shelf-reading be done at least once a month so that all volumes in the entire collection will be in correct classified order. To the user a misshelved book is equivalent to a lost book. If no use occurs because a book is improperly shelved (and thus not accessible to the user) such a title is likely to be weeded under the shelf-time period criterion. Whether this weakens the collection appreciably needs to be examined more closely.

That use data be recorded and preserved as carefully as is reasonably possible. This means that circulation desk personnel must be careful and accurate when charging books in and out. This objective has been included for two reasons.

It is obvious that careless data will cause the weeding of volumes or materials that should not be weeded and the keeping of other materials that should have been weeded. Careless data control can destroy the validity of this whole procedure.

Secondly, in a field study of circulation control made by the author in 1973, a check of the quality of the work being done uncovered hundreds of errors. Unless people realize the importance of careful work and unless they are trained and supervised, the level of performance is likely to be poor.

That books from locked and inaccessible collections, which are to be weeded, be placed upon the open shelves or in primary storage areas before a decision is made on their removal from the collection. It was found, as might be expected, that such materials are not able to compete for user attention with the rest of the collection. If weeding is contemplated, the books should be tested in the marketplace of normal use.

A study in depth of books located in restricted storage areas showed that usage was one-fourth that of similar titles located on open shelves.[1] Perhaps the restricted books should be returned to open stacks since such restrictions reduce their value. The purpose of relocating books is defensive: to prevent the discarding of books that would have been identified as being part of the core if they had been stored differently.

The reshelving period should not be less than a shelf-time that would be represented by a circulation shelf-time period to include 95 percent of the future use, or whatever other percentage might have been predetermined for the keeping level.

That weeding be done immediately after the signal for weeding has been received. If this is not done, the non-core collection starts to be identified as part of the core collection, destroying much of the value of this system.

That libraries establish written objectives yearly which relate to the purposes of weeding. Weeding can be done for many reasons, and the exact reasons become important in the decision-making processes involved in the weeding procedures. When the library's greater goals are clearly defined, levels of weeding or non-weeding become easier to determine.

That libraries should annually establish the exact level of future use to be retained by the present collection. This can be determined for the library as a whole or for individual parts of the collection. The decision should be made in advance.

For example, if purchasing of new biographies is to be heavy, one might reasonably decide that keeping 90 percent of the future use of this collection will be adequate to fulfill the greater objective of retaining biography use at its present level.

That the public card catalog be weeded annually so that it more nearly reflects the library's holdings. This also implies that shelf-lists and other listings be kept up to date. This is a necessary step if collections are to have adequate and accurate catalog accessibility and are to reflect more accurately the library's collection.

Implicit in the need for weeding of catalogs is the necessity of periodic book inventories.

That inventory be taken at least once a year and unintentional gaps in the collection be filled in. Since the suggested criterion for weeding is past use, the absence of books from the collection due to theft or loss will result in distorted shelf-time data for remaining works and the core collection concept will be distorted. The distortion of data works in two ways.

First, a missing volume affects use of other works. If a user seeks information in a volume that is missing (the preferred work), he may look for the information in another book. That book, which ordinarily might not have had a recorded use, will now show a use at the expense of the preferred volume.

Second, it is impossible to know if a lost book should be identified as part of the core collection.

Therefore, it must be recognized that, since data can be collected only for books in the existing collection, it is necessary for the library to attempt to replace missing books meant to be in the collection.

If Volume 2 of the *World Book Encyclopedia* were lost, it would be recognized that the entire set was an integral part of the collection and the missing volume would be replaced. Subjective judgment is called for in determining which books to replace in the collection in the absence of shelf-time data, but it is the same judgment used in the initial ordering of new books, which is a normal part of the book selection process.

That libraries keep records on characteristics of the collection or the library that directly affect the use of materials, thereby altering the composition of the core collection. It is apparent that while use is the best predictor of core collections, many things affect usage.

Use is affected by accessibility, location in the library, height of the shelves, seasonal variations, appearance of the volumes, form of the materials, special shelving, librarians' recommendations, special promotion, bibliographies, dust covers, loan periods, reserved collections, etc. As an objective, it is suggested that each library keep records for one year on some variable and quantify its effect upon usage. Such variables that affect usage, were they known, could help to maximize circulation, to change the composition of the core collection (perhaps by making it smaller), and to produce a knowledge base replacing the intuitive base now used by librarians for many decisions. For example, if books at eye-level are used more than books on top and bottom shelves, the core collections, if kept in their present locations, will still satisfy the predicted future use; however, the core collection and the library will not have maximized the usage of the total collection. If such collections were on shelves which somehow could change their relative positions from time to time, a different and more satisfactory core collection would be likely.[2] One solution might be that no books should be stored on shelves where the location adversely affects book use.

A special set of problems besets university libraries. The impact of reserve collections, restricted collections, multiple library locations (departmental and undergraduate libraries, for instance), changes in curriculum, special assignments, long-term loan periods to faculty, all might affect the core collection concept. Yale University reports that their 4,000,000 volumes can be found in 64 different places,[3] and the University of Oxford, England, owns more volumes and has even more physical locations for them (72).

SUMMARY

The purpose of these objectives is to clarify exactly what a library wishes to do about weeding and to make weeding easier and more valid. The objectives for weeding listed above should be chosen to coincide with each library's goals. The sub-objectives begin to offer a method for meaningful weeding.

REFERENCES

1.   Stanley James Slote, "The Predictive Value of Past-Use Patterns of Adult Fiction in Public Libraries for Identifying Core Collections" (unpublished Ph.D. dissertation, Rutgers University, 1970). University Microfilms, Inc., Ann Arbor, Michigan, No. 71-3104, p. 116.

2.   Stacks that revolve in such a way that shelf-positions keep changing are now found in some book stores. Their purpose is to prevent shelf location from adversely affecting sales.

3.   Lee Ash, *Yale's Selective Book Retirement Program* (Hamden, Conn.: Archon Books, 1963), p. xi.

CHAPTER 6

WEEDING METHODS USED IN LIBRARIES

APPROACHES TO WEEDING

A number of different general approaches to weeding have been given serious attention. These are:

Subjective weeding. This method involves a series of rules, principles, or guides that require for implementation subjective judgment on the part of the weeder. This is the most common form of weeding found in libraries today.

Age. With this method of weeding, books are removed from the shelves according to the date of imprint, copyright, or acquisition. Such age data are often used to assist decision-making when doing subjective weeding. Future usage patterns can be reliably predicted when age is used as a criterion.

Shelf-time period. The length of time a book remains unused on the shelf between circulations is called its shelf-time period. This method is often used intuitively together with subjective criteria.

Mathematical approaches. Several complex formulas or models have been suggested which, in fact, utilize information covered by the methods listed above. To date, these have been theoretical suggestions of questionable validity.

Combined criteria. The use of shelf-time period and imprint date, or any other combination of criteria, has been investigated and utilized in weeding. Such combinations have not been found to improve the quality of weeding.

PROBLEMS ENCOUNTERED USING
THESE APPROACHES

Each of these approaches presents serious difficulties. The following is an attempt to outline the problems.

Subjective weeding. When weeding using subjective criteria, the weeder has selected criteria satisfactory to himself but unsubstantiated by objective evidence. If two experienced weeders are given the same collection to weed, widely differing collections of weedable volumes are likely to be identified.

In addition, the procedure is a lengthy one. Since weeding is considered to be a professional task, it is left, in small libraries especially, to a professional who already has many other responsibilities. It is not uncommon that the weeding procedure may take two or three years in a public library. It is also not uncommon, under these circumstances, that a weeding program has been started and left unfinished when enthusiasm has flagged. The methodology in subjective weeding is to make up rules that *seem* rational and apply them in a way that *seems* reasonable.

Imprint age. When using age as a criterion for weeding, several decisions must be made before weeding can start. It must be decided what date is to be used. The following are some of the dates that can be employed:

1. Copyright date. The date used can be the earliest, the most recent, or an average of these two dates. It can be a date reflecting a major reworking of a title, a revised edition, or a new edition.

2. Imprint date. Here again the date used may be the first or last imprint date of a volume. Sometimes no copyright of a work exists and the only date available is the imprint date.

3. Purchase or acquisition date. If the "newness" of a volume is to be judged by some date, the purchase date or acquisition date could give more accurate information than copyright or imprint dates for the collection in question.

An even more reasonable date would be the date the book was shelved. It has been suggested that when using the book card system of circulation control, the original shelving date be the first date entered on the card. Such dating would simplify subsequent data interpretation.

4. Date originally written or published. This date reflects the age of a work but not the age of a volume. If more newly created works are the ones that are used most, such a date might well be significant. However, newer editions of classics tend to be used more than older, especially as type face and size improves.

5. Some other date. A date that a volume is rebound, for example, might be of significance.

Once the desired date is selected two serious questions remain. What date is to be used if a title is to have all of its volumes considered together? Where does one find the date desired, and is it a practical source? The problem of multiple volumes for one title is not serious if these are different editions and are treated as separate works. Generally, a new edition of a classic will be preferred to an older edition. Therefore, it is advisable to consider volumes independently rather than as a group.

However, if all similar titles are to be considered together, the decision of which date to use becomes a major problem, since a weeding decision might be hard to apply. There does not appear to be a satisfactory solution of this difficulty.

The difficulty in determining what date to use manifests itself in other ways. If titles are to be considered as a group, all of the copies of the same title held by the library must be uncovered. The card catalog or shelf-list will be the authority but will not indicate that a cataloged volume has been stolen or otherwise removed from its normal place. In addition to reading the shelves, all date-due records will have to be checked. If the volume itself lacks dates, a bibliographic search to determine when it was written, printed, or published will be required.

Shelf-time period. There are at least four methods of developing shelf-time period (discussed in detail in Chapter 13) and each of these has its problems both in the development of the criterion and in its application. What follows is a selective summary. The appendices detail some of the problems.

1. *Shelf-time periods developed from book cards.* The book card system of circulation control presents a number of problems. The cards generally reflect the date a book is due, not the dates borrowed or returned, and therefore shelf-time periods are not clearly indicated. When book cards are lost or used up and discarded, information is lacking. When information is given only for circulating volumes, it is difficult and time-consuming to create comparable data for non-circulating books.

2. *Shelf-time periods developed by marking spines.* When using this method, confidence in the data is weakened by the difficulties of controlling the accuracy of the spine marking. The physical markings can be removed, obscured, or overlooked. Careless or disinterested personnel at the circulation desk can fail to make the proper marks. The spine marking system is valuable, however, in that books can be weeded without opening them up or inspecting them in any other way.

This system is generally most useful with libraries using the transaction card system or some other comparable charging system. Some charging systems now print a small colored dot on the back of the book card simultaneously with recording the needed charge-out data. Changing the color of the dot differentiates between months or years.

The spine marking system is applicable to the non-circulating collection in libraries where all volumes used within the library could be spine-marked and reshelved by library personnel.

3. *Short-cut method.* This method assumes that all volumes under two years old are in the core collection. Their book cards need not be inspected. The use of this technique for actual weeding could be further simplified by the regular inclusion of imprint dates along with call numbers on the spines of all volumes. The newer books could be left in the core collection; the book card would not need to be examined. This technique, which is useful only when the book card method of circulation is being used, is a simplification of method 1 above.

4. *Computer methods.* It is possible that for libraries using a computer circulation control system, programs could be developed to give print-outs of all the shelf-time periods of all the volumes that have circulated. This data could be manipulated further to report the cut-off date. Needless to say, the program, the print-out, and the hardware are expensive. Such a method of weeding has been suggested in the literature but has never been used. Nonetheless, it could be a valuable by-product of such a circulation system.

Mathematical approaches. The mathematical approach involves quantifying certain variables and computing them in a specified formula or equation. The method is difficult to understand and to apply, and the data are difficult to uncover; complex mathematics is misused in this situation. Morse[1] and Lister[2] both recommend this approach but since their orientation is toward ultimate storage and comparative use costs, their method has more validity when applied to cost control than when applied to weeding.

Further, in the use of mathematical models, the accepted assumptions are quantified to give percentages, costs, or other specific units upon which to make decisions. From a practical point of view, these mathematical results tend to be far from reality, since, in general, a whole series of assumptions (themselves unproved and often untested) are quantified. The combining of a series of *assumptions* to give precise mathematical results is considered to be an invalid approach.

For example, certain of these formulas assume that, on the average, obsolescence increases with age. While this may be true, *on the average*, assuming a steady rate of obsolescence and using it in a decision-making formula compounds the error. Individual volumes differ from average behavior. A formula produced in this manner will lend an unjustified confidence to decision-making.

REFERENCES

1. Philip M. Morse, *Library Effectiveness: A Systems Approach* (Cambridge, Mass.: M.I.T. Press, 1968).

2. Winston Charles Lister, "Least Cost Decision Rules for the Selection of Library Materials for Compact Storage" (unpublished Ph.D. dissertation, Purdue University, 1967).

CHAPTER 7

CORE COLLECTIONS FOR
SPECIFIC TYPES OF LIBRARIES

INTRODUCTION

The following are some ideas that might prove helpful in creating the core collection percentage figures for different kinds of libraries and different types of materials. What percentage of present use should one aim to keep? It must be emphasized that the higher the use-percentage kept, the smaller the amount of weeded material. Nevertheless, even at the level of keeping 100 percent of the future use of a collection, weeding will still be indicated.

It is not easy to establish "keeping" percentages. The basic difficulty is that all of these percentages are based in part upon subjective judgment and are subject to change based upon experience.

SMALL PUBLIC LIBRARIES

By "small public libraries" is meant libraries that do not feel that they are the permanent storage centers for the world's heritage. They frequently have limited reference collections and minimal reference services. Typical are hundreds of big city branch libraries and the libraries in many cities of under 20,000 population. Their services are basically threefold: they supply recreational and informational reading to their clients; they serve as a supplement to the public school educational program; and they supply a limited number of reference works. The quality of the reference service is low and the present patterns are such that 85 to 90 percent of the requests are for ready reference or simple reference questions.[1] Thus, small public libraries are performing a wide range of partial or low-level services, which society accepts.

Therefore, the core collection can be subdivided into rather broad areas without exposing society to great inconvenience. Limited experience in several such libraries indicates that weeding with four separate collection divisions is adequate. These four consist of:

1. Fiction, including mysteries, short stories, science fiction, and westerns.

2. Non-fiction; all the Dewey classification combined as one class. Biographies are also included here.

39

3. Reference materials, including periodicals, newspapers, pamphlets, photographs, and other miscellaneous materials.

4. Archives; anything in the permanent collection. Each of these areas tends to have shelf-time periods differing significantly from the others, yet within each group a certain reasonable consistency exists.

One might start by trying to retain 95 percent of the present usage for fiction, 97 percent for non-fiction, and 99 percent for reference; archives would not be weeded at all, except as the objectives of this collection might change.

A small project was undertaken by the author to observe the effect of combining fiction and non-fiction into one collection for weeding purposes, even though the weeding was not actually performed. It was decided to keep 97 percent of the anticipated future circulation. The impact on the separate classes was not unexpected. In the library studied over 99 percent of the fiction use and about 93 percent of the non-fiction used would have been retained.

Furthermore, non-fiction would have had to be weeded more extensively than fiction. This result was not as disturbing as might at first appear. Fiction is likely to have a much longer useful life and be more valid as it gets older. Non-fiction (textbooks, for example) tend to be full of untruths a few years after publication. In an average small public library there are hundreds of classics in fiction but only a handful of useful classics in non-fiction.

Another aspect of small library weeding is that such weeding is unlikely to do much harm. The sale, donation, relocation, or destruction of the weeded collection has few dangers. However, it is suggested that special regional libraries be given an opportunity to add these weeded volumes to their permanent collections. An occasional volume may fill a gap in such a larger collection. It is also suggested that regional libraries make their collections more widely available to the average reader.

MAJOR PUBLIC LIBRARY RESEARCH COLLECTIONS

Much of what has been said about smaller public libraries also relates to those massive and outstanding research libraries that have developed in major urban areas. These include such libraries as the John Crear in Chicago, Enoch Pratt in Baltimore, the Newark Public Library, and many other large libraries located in the bigger cities. They are frequently trying to perform two distinct functions.

One function is to serve as the popular public library, satisfying a number of recreational, educational, and ready reference functions. In these areas, weeding may follow the general pattern of the small public library. In the *Five Library Study* it was found that an outstanding collection, such as that of Newark, had lower circulation figures in fiction than the smaller collection in the Morristown, N.J., Public Library, which contained one-quarter the number of fiction volumes. Insofar as it operates as a local circulator of popular materials, weeding can keep 95 to 99 percent of the anticipated future use without denying the patron what he wants.

The second important function, that of a regional resource and reference center, calls for the use of higher keeping levels for the core collection or perhaps a different approach to weeding. For example, in a regional resource center it is likely that none of the books should be discarded unless they are either duplicates or are being replaced with the same or similar material. Furthermore, much of the material being weeded might well be retained in secondary storage areas. It is good practice to determine in advance the number of duplicates that are to be retained. Some libraries protect their collections by retaining two copies of a title.

Reference and information collections may have even greater limitations put upon them. Depending upon the level of the reference services it is called upon to perform, no weeding should be done except for replacing certain works with newer editions or more definitive works. Even here, out-of-date editions often become important resources.

However, with massive research and reference collections, it is frequently the case that one part of the collection is more accessible than other parts. Often a closed stack area exists. The weeding procedure may then identify reference works that are likely candidates to be removed from the open stacks and re-established in the closed stack area. Certainly for important, large, heavily used reference collections, the core collection should satisfy at least 99.5 to 100 percent of the anticipated use.

MEDIUM-SIZED PUBLIC LIBRARIES

Little information needs to be added for those libraries that fall between the above two groups. Many medium-sized centralized libraries are characterized by a dual role of the major library; often the branches are the popular circulation libraries and the downtown central branch is a resource and reference center. The degree to which these libraries are used should determine the characteristics of the core collections. As with major resource centers, the library might be more interested in replacing lost and stolen books than in weeding out current holdings. The usage, objectives, and client expectancy should help determine weeding levels.

Where public libraries of any size have divided subject responsibility for collections or have specialized collections of value, it is obvious that weeding must be considered in the light of the library's goals.

PUBLIC SCHOOL LIBRARIES

It is the often-stated objective of school libraries that they support the curriculum of the school. Other goals involve services to staff, administrators, and parents. In actuality, many of these libraries are used mostly as study halls, and the understaffing of these libraries has been notorious.

Basically, school libraries are acting as self-service supermarkets and their direct services hardly touch the individual student. As Berelson pointed out, only 40 percent of the books children borrow come from the school library.[2]

Of all the types of libraries, school libraries lend themselves most to weeding. However, they are the most reluctant to remove out-of-date and unused materials. In the face of their overwhelming problem of undersupport, school libraries have failed to prevent the landslide of students from descending upon the public library. As courses and syllabuses change, as new subjects appear and old disappear, as students' interests and awareness broaden, great challenges are presented to school libraries.

The fact that school libraries are able to accept only a limited part of the responsibility means that they can be weeded in depth without seriously affecting the users. Collections and services are defective and will continue to be inadequate until school libraries have eight or ten times their present resources. They do not have any responsibility to preserve the national heritage, to be definitive research resource centers, or to be complete or comprehensive in any area.

As far as the recreational collections are concerned, it is suggested that school libraries try to retain 90 percent of anticipated future use and buy heavily to build up greater usage, since what is newest is what tends to have the greatest demand.

In the area of the reference collection, 95 percent is adequate, since supplemental collections are to be used anyway. Even the most perfunctory look at school libraries reinforces the opinion that deep weeding would improve collections.

One of the advantages a school library has in developing weeding criteria is that one year's use patterns are generally adequate for prediction unless new courses have been added to the curriculum. Conversely, lack of use in one year is often the first indication to the librarian that a course has been dropped. The one-year natural cycle means that the weeding criteria can almost always be developed within one year without worrying about long-range cyclical influences. This is a characteristic not found in other types of libraries, with the possible exception of undergraduate college libraries.

JUNIOR COLLEGE LIBRARIES

Everything said about the school library might be considered valid to some degree for the junior college library. In general, the main problem here is in building up, rather than reducing, the size of the collection. Since many of these libraries are new, less weeding may be called for. In addition, weeding seems to present less risk than in other libraries, for two reasons.

In the first place, a large number of courses generate relatively little use of library material. This may be a result of the more practical nature of the terminal courses. These libraries have only a very small influence on a large segment of their students.

Secondly, the yearly cycle helps to accelerate decision-making and adds confidence in identifying materials not likely to be used again. Thus, a reasonable standard for core collections would be one that would satisfy between 90 percent and 95 percent of the anticipated future use. To date, no important research project on weeding has treated school or junior college libraries.

COLLEGE AND UNIVERSITY LIBRARIES

The focus of most weeding research has been upon college and university libraries, since this is where many of the most serious problems exist.

Many such libraries have had critical space shortages because they lack the financial resources necessary for expansion. Rapid growth of the major universities (and their libraries), financial pressures due to increased costs and decreased donations, increase in the number of advanced degrees awarded, and recent cutbacks of government support have forced these libraries to seek relief.

For years university libraries have projected the image of the collectors and preservers of knowledge. It is not true, however, that these libraries are solely repositories of the great national and human heritage. Collections of old textbooks, workbooks, out-of-date and useless non-fiction, low quality gift-books, and books that have never been used at all abound in most of these collections. Therefore, it is suggested that in non-research collections, such as fiction, textbooks, etc., weeding be done as it is elsewhere, keeping in the core collection those works likely to retain 95 percent of their future usage.

In the remainder of the collection, weeding can be applied at any reasonable level, since transfer from primary to secondary storage should be the basic form of disposition of non-core works. Where no other factors are involved, the 99 percent future use level is recommended.

One other kind of weeding of main collections is possible. When departments have independent or geographically decentralized collections, it is possible to remove a complete section of the main library to such separated libraries in the system. Of course, such action must be based upon clear-cut objectives relating to the ease of access desired and the resources of money, space, and personnel available. Duplication of collections in the main branch and its departmental libraries is expensive, but it improves the access dramatically.

The overlapping nature of modern disciplines and the interdisciplinary character of many courses complicate the solutions to easy access. Departmental libraries increase accessibility to some and reduce it to others, unless considerable duplication of materials exists.

Even in monolothic libraries, where no departmental libraries exist, materials are scattered rather widely. This occurs because of types of format (books, oversized books, pamphlets, microfilm, periodicals, AV materials); age of material (different runs for older materials); new book displays; archival collections; condition or state of processing (new books, periodicals being bound, books partially cataloged, temporarily lost volumes, etc.); special needs (reserve collections, circulating and non-circulating collections, government documents); and divisions within one library. One can logically locate similar subjects in dozens of different places in a large library—a fact that reduces easy access. When duplication is used to facilitate access, the space problem worsens.

Since "easy accessibility" does not seem to be a major objective in many of the massive libraries, secondary storage may have little serious effect on the overall level of service. Use of secondary storage might well increase accessibility to the primary collection to such a degree that overall service is improved.

While generally a 99 percent core collection keeping level is called for, weeding in much greater depth is not completely out of the question. The weeding level for these libraries may be determined by other practical considerations. It may be that the number of volumes currently held in primary storage completely fills up the library, so that no additional space is available. Instead of predetermining the keeping level on the basis of usage, one can determine the number of volumes to be retained in the primary storage area stacks, and accept whatever level of future use this will produce.

For example, if the Briarcliff Public Library needed to get along with 70 percent of the present shelving space, it would keep 98 percent of its present usage.[3] The secondary storage areas available could be used for determining such levels. There should not be more books transferred to secondary storage than can be stored conveniently. The size of the core collection may also be decided by determining the most economic mix of primary and secondary storage, considering all the costs involved for book removal, library maintenance, cost of services, etc.

As large libraries grow, these more practical considerations can be taken into account and careful research should be undertaken to help in the decision-making processes.

SPECIAL LIBRARIES

Librarianship in general has been hurt by attempting to group a large miscellaneous, dissimilar group of libraries into one class and calling them "special libraries." At best, there is a very tenuous similarity between the various types of special libraries. How do large legal libraries relate to small stock photography libraries? How do hospital, music, and newspaper libraries interrelate? Their materials, staff, size, objectives, and services frequently bear no visible relationships.

It is suggested that the various types of libraries might create their own concepts of core collections. Even within individual types, sub-types would be required. Clearly, then, each library must be considered in terms of its objectives—those relating both to its materials and services, and to the alternatives available.

For example, some newspaper libraries not only clip and file their own newspaper but also index it. Obviously, older clippings can be weeded with much less exposure when an index exists.

Criteria can be developed. National news, well indexed and reported elsewhere, can be weeded in depth without exposure. The general technique advocated here, that of anticipated use, can still be valuable and is perhaps the best approach to creating weeding criteria for special libraries.

In one weeded library, 100 percent of anticipated future use was accepted, and still 90 percent of the items were in the non-core collection.[4] Most special libraries lend themselves to weeding in depth, even though generalized keeping levels are hard to recommend for special libraries as a group.

As with archives, the objectives often prevent weeding of special materials on the basis of shelf-time period. One example was found by the author in a music publisher's library, where all copyrighted songs, sheet music, records, original manuscripts, etc., were retained. This was the stock in trade of the main business, and legal or financial matters could arise from any music holding, no matter how long its shelf-time period.

LIBRARY SYSTEMS

Ideally, public library systems have the advantage that certain centralized services can make weeding in depth less threatening to the integrity of the combined collections. Centralized or regional resource centers could be responsible for holding unique but little-used volumes.

Perhaps the best tool to encourage weeding is a union catalog. The easy accessibility of works at a neighbor's library reduces the need to hold many questionable volumes. When union catalogs are combined with telephone interlibrary loan and pick up and delivery service, members of systems often take on some of the characteristics of branches, and they can weed at the 90 to 95 percent use level.

SUMMARY

The purpose of this chapter is to give some guidelines for determining the acceptable level of use retained by core collections. It can be seen that librarians must use considerable judgment, experience, and professionalism in achieving this.

Under the proposed methods, these judgments are limited to judgments of objectives, goals, and services to be given rather than individual titles to be saved or weeded. At the worst, it gives us two groups of books: the core collection, from which *no* volumes will be weeded, and the non-core collection, from which *all* the weeded volumes will be selected.

Real judgment is also essential in disposing of the weeded volumes, in evaluating secondary storage, and in following up on the success of a weeding program. This total approach does not lower the professionalism of librarianship, but raises it. It replaces the present primitive technique of selecting titles or volumes for weeding with a quantified criterion, created through objective observation.

REFERENCES

1. William A. Katz, *Introduction to Reference Work, Vol. II: Reference Services* (New York: McGraw-Hill, 1969), p. 38.

2. Bernard Berelson, *The Library's Public* (New York: Columbia University Press, 1949), p. 11.

3. Stanley James Slote, "The Predictive Value of Past-Use Patterns of Adult Fiction in Public Libraries for Identifying Core Collections" (unpublished Ph.D. dissertation, Rutgers University, 1970). University Microfilms, Inc., Ann Arbor, Michigan, No. 71-3104, p. 79.

4. Stanley J. Slote, "An Approach to Weeding Criteria for Newspaper Libraries," *American Documentation* XIX (April 1968), p. 172.

Part 2

Research Projects and
Weeding Methods
Summarized

CHAPTER 8

ANALYSIS AND REVIEW OF THE
LITERATURE OF WEEDING

PURPOSES FOR A STUDY
OF THE LITERATURE

There has been a massive quantity of material published on the subject of library weeding. Almost 1,000 use studies can be identified, if one adds the more current works to Jain's list of 631 works.[1] From this mass there have been selected reports that add substance to the specific approaches used in this book. These selected reports represent the background for the present work, which has attempted to take another step forward.

The purpose or motivation behind the production of a book or article often becomes rather clear upon reading it. Its purpose affects its tone and content. There are many reasons for studying or adding to the literature of a subject:

To compare what one is doing with what is being done elsewhere in the field.

To look for hard facts—real evidence that would cause one to reinforce or discard certain accepted techniques.

To uncover limitations of the knowledge in a field in order to undertake research, starting from the present knowledge base.

To examine the suggestions of thinkers in the field, in order to give direction to further thought and study.

To read of the experience of others as a guide to identifying pitfalls to be avoided.

To find out specifically how to perform certain operations.

To keep current with the literature.

To create new knowledge in the field.

CRITICISM OF LIBRARY LITERATURE

Two characteristics of the literature in librarianship (and weeding in particular) are that there is no cumulation of knowledge, and that there is no consistency in the objectives of the overall literature in the field. Current articles frequently show no knowledge of the history and past thought in the subject. It is a serious criticism of the literature of librarianship, including the more than 700 periodicals in the field, that articles currently appearing could have been written 15 to 75 years ago. Editors accept such articles without limitation or discrimination.

What is needed is not only the publication of the first stirrings of new knowledge, hard facts, tendencies and information gained from experiment, and careful observation, but also a willingness on the part of readers to accept what is known.[2] It has been known for at least 13 years that shelf-time period is the best criterion for identifying core collections. Yet, many articles and books published in the years since do not accept this finding, which apparently has been one of the best-kept secrets in librarianship.

The first criticism of the literature of librarianship concerning weeding, core collections, and shelf-time period is that the literature has had no impact on the practitioners, teachers, and leaders in the field. It is possible that the very mass of publications has blocked the view of what is significant.

What is *needed* are facts, data, or ideas that will stimulate the serious student or the practitioner to better his performance and enlarge his knowledge in the field. The following section makes an attempt to classify some of the literature. What has been said about the literature of weeding might well be repeated for almost any topic in librarianship.

CHARACTERISTICS OF THE LITERATURE

In much of the literature of weeding and library usage, there is a similarity in the type of works published year after year. In general, these types of works can be characterized as follows:

Repetitive. Repetition can be one of three kinds—either the actual reprint of an article that has been published before; summaries or analysis of previous works; or a fresh presentation of what has been said before, with little credit given to the originator. While a certain amount of repetition might be helpful for the learning process, librarians have been bombarded with repetitions of the same old, and perhaps invalid, ideas for 100 years.

"How-to" literature. "How-to" articles are generally authoritative but give little evidence, few facts, and no sources. A better way to do something is claimed, even though it is frequently a method that has been alternately recommended or rejected throughout the decades! The ultimate authority is personal judgment, often not even supported by a simple literature search or by the most basic attempts to compare two different techniques. One interesting characteristic of this kind of work is the conflict and disagreement that it creates among the authorities.

Scholarly historical summary. Such work is generally a carefully documented study of the past literature of the subject, usually selective, in order to emphasize the development of the field and the best practices. This kind of article has form, meaning, and usually a good point. It is a short-cut for a new student in the field, and might be considered a guide to the best literature of a subject.

Broad philosophy. This is an attempt to synthesize past knowledge and to reinforce newer valid concepts. It always has some strong base for the concepts contained, often the most recent research reports or new technologies (computers and advanced math, for example). This approach tends to make its points in an organized way, as contrasted to the authoritative approaches.

Controlled study. A controlled study is a carefully planned, scholarly attempt to uncover new knowledge. It is a scientific, experimental approach with enough of the data, background, methodology, and techniques reported so that the experiment can be replicated. It uses the "scientific method," with an attempt to observe one variable at a time. The conclusions follow directly from the data, and the range of their reliability is clearly defined. Where variables are not being manipulated by the researcher, an attempt is made to be unobtrusive and avoid having the observation affect the results. Usually the claims made for the findings are modest. Several such controlled studies relating to weeding will follow in the next chapters.

PROBLEMS IN THE APPLICATION
OF THE LITERATURE

The literature of weeding is characterized by a number of other general problems:

1. There is a great variety in the quality, style, and value of the articles. This mix, even within the confines of one publication, must make one wary about the quality of the editing of even the best of the scholarly journals.

2. In general, there has been a lack of cumulative study in the field. Strangely, there is a certain amount of repetition and replication of each of the new techniques that have been reported, as if no one ever starts where the last researcher left off. Nor have the researchers themselves seemed to develop knowledge banks of increased information.

3. Access to the literature through bibliographies and indexes is difficult, inefficient, and incomplete.

4. Very few reports are complete. Fragmentation is common. Articles omitting data, techniques, background, or meanings are the norm. The reader is unable to tell whether what has been omitted was invalid, was left undone, or was omitted by carelessness.

5. There is much opinion and little hard knowledge in the literature. A wide range of periodicals avoid articles with data, research, statistics, and methodology as being "too academic."

SUMMARY OF THE LITERATURE
OF WEEDING

Criteria used. In general, the studies that follow have used two principle criteria: 1) the age of a volume, and 2) the length of time a volume remains in the library between successive uses (or the number of uses in a given period of time).

Various dates have been used to represent the age of a volume: the publication date, the year of accession, and the copyright date. In addition, the language of the publication and its country of origin have been used as variables.

The above variables have also been used in combinations. However, shelf-time period has the most serious support, with respect to both the number of supporters and the validity of the research evidence.

Methods of recreating use patterns. There has been some discussion in the literature as to how to uncover the past patterns of book use in a library. Most of the studies relied upon the book cards for their information; several reconstructed the information needed during the study, with no reference to past records; often, a combination of these methods was used. Two major approaches have been suggested for reconstructing circulation patterns as described by shelf-time periods.

1. The "historical reconstruction" approach is an attempt to record, in terms of the chosen variable, the entire use pattern of a volume since its acquisition in a library. When this method has been used, however, most researchers have limited their study to the last several years of use.

The weakness of this method is that much of the important data may be missing. Cards from well-used books are often filled up and discarded, books are lost or stolen along with their book cards, charging systems are changed, and cards replaced. In general, the information available might be very unreliable.

2. The "current circulation" method looks at a very recent period of circulation (usually the most recent few days or weeks) and assumes that the present pattern of use at circulation is a valid sample of the total use pattern. Several such samples of circulation may be taken over a period of time and compared for consistency.

The weaknesses here are that seasonal patterns might not show up, and that there are other factors that might make a short-term sample unrepresentative of the whole pattern. School assignments can change; different days of the week may have different use patterns; and the relative use (the percentage of the whole class represented by the sample) is disregarded. The "current circulation" method has become more and more the preferred method with recent researchers.

Aims of the studies. The scope of the studies was often restricted by the aim of the work, especially in the area of validating findings relating to weeding. Attempts were often made to find weeding criteria useful in identifying core collections.

However, studies were also made in order to justify automated circulation methods, to compute and compare the cost of various kinds of primary and secondary storage, to evaluate collections, to test mathematical formula, and to limit the growth of active collections stored in the primary collection area. Therefore, the studies vary tremendously in their emphasis or lack of emphasis on weeding and its usefulness.

Findings of the studies. There have been a wide range of findings, and certain conflicting results have been reported.

1. In general, shelf-time period was found to be the most acceptable variable for identifying core collections. The methodologies and assumptions were often validated with strong evidence for the superiority of the shelf-time period variable in predicting future use. Most studies agreed that this is the most valuable variable revealed.

2. The age of the volume was found to be somewhat predictive of future use, but generally of little practical value. Basically, the rejection of a small number of older volumes—the classics, which circulate with patterns similar to those of newer books—causes the age of volumes to be an inferior predictor of the future use.

3. Several explanations were found as to why shelf-time period produced a smaller core collection than the age of a volume.

4. Techniques for uncovering the information needed to produce weeding criteria have been simplified and improved. The early serious studies, which involved tedious investigation of the old book cards, have given way to the present, simpler techniques of marking spines.

5. Objective weeding was frequently recommended as a replacement for the judgment or subjective weeding most commonly used. Wherever controlled testing has been undertaken, the objective criteria have proven to be as valid as or more valid than subjective weeding.

6. No examples could be found where weeding was based solely on objective criteria; in every case some subjective criteria were added, often as an afterthought. Apparently it was emotionally difficult to weed using only objective criteria.

7. The problems of the growth of collections and the need for weeding were highlighted in almost every study. Weeding always appeared to be the solution, yet few reported that it had solved long-term shelf-space needs. Nor have any libraries reported a consistent *long-term* weeding effort.

THE LITERATURE REVIEWED

An attempt was made to uncover information about the use of fiction, since the *Five Library Study*, which is the basis of this book, was done with *fiction* alone. Unfortunately, very little research had been done with fiction. It was found, however, that no matter what types of books or collections were observed, shelf-time period was by far the best predictor of future use.

These reports have been divided into two groups—those based on judgment, which, in retrospect, proved to be valid judgment; and those based on research. The first group of studies has identified the problems that encourage weeding and has recommended approaches that have been later validated.

Studies identifying the problems.

1. **Eliot, Charles W.** The need for a criterion for thinning has long been a subject for discussion. Charles William Eliot, president of Harvard, outlined in 1902 the problems faced by university libraries.[3] After mentioning the rapid growth of libraries, he says:

Under these conditions the great need of means of discrim-
inating between books which may fairly be said to be in use and
books which may fairly be said to be not in use has been forced on
me, . . .[4]

I admit at once that the means of just discrimination between
books in use and books not in use are not easy to discern or to
apply; . . .[5]

The concept in his first statement has been repeated many times in the
literature. He has hinted at the idea of using objective weeding criteria.

Thus, it might naturally be suspected that a book which had
not been called for in a university library for twenty years possessed
but a faint vitality; . . .[6]

2. **Ranck, Samuel.** In 1911, Samuel Ranck reported on a study he had
made at the Grand Rapids Public Library,[7] one of the few use studies made in a
public library. He stated the problem from the library administrator's point of
view:

Every circulating library of considerable magnitude that has
been in operation for a number of years gradually accumulates many
volumes that are seldom or never used.[8]

He then presented data showing the "time since last use" for all the
64,162 volumes in the library. Among his findings were that 20 percent of the
books had not circulated at all during the previous two years and 10 percent had
not circulated in the previous five years. What is of particular interest is the
similarity of his findings of more than 60 years ago compared with more recent
findings (see Table 2). His 15.1 percent of fiction non-circulators compares
closely to the figures of 12.1, 15.0, and 12.6 percent found for Briarcliff,
Tarrytown, and Morristown collections of the *Five Library Study* (see
Chapter 10).

He pointed out the need for use studies:

This problem of the unused book is one that will increase as
the library grows older, and I believe that we cannot undertake the
solution of it too soon or too carefully.[9]

3. **Ash, Lee.** Ash's report[10] is a summary of extensive and detailed
studies made at Yale during a three-year period. It is an example of a
middle-of-the-road study that followed both the folklore and the science of
weeding. The study, which was used to establish practical guidelines for "the
selective retirement program," combined objective weeding criteria with
judgment and library expertise. Some of the conclusions parallel those of later
and more detailed studies.

Table 2

COMPARISON OF DATA
RANCK 1911 VS. SLOTE 1969 COLLECTION CHARACTERISTICS

	Ranck	Briarcliff	Tarrytown	Morristown	Trenton	Newark
% of *fiction* not circulating in last two years	15.1	12.1	15.0	12.6	44.2	37.1

% Previously Charged Out

| Shelf-Time Period | Total Collection | Fiction Only | | | | |
		Briarcliff	Tarrytown	Morristown	Trenton	Newark
24 months	79.2*	87.9	85.0	87.4	55.8	62.9
60 months	90.4	99.7	96.8	96.5	73.5	82.7
120 months	95.8	100.0	98.9	97.7	82.8	92.9
204 months	98.6	-	99.8	100.0	92.2	98.0
300 months	99.0	-	100.0	-	97.2	99.8
312 months and over	100.0	-	-	-	100.0	100.0

*Figure for fiction was 84.9%.

> If a book has been charged out on an average of once a year or more for the past five years, it should be considered "heavily used" material and should not be transferred . . .[11]

This criterion of *repetitive* use to identify core collections is not commonplace in the literature of weeding. Most of the studies have shown that a use once in five years (rather than once a year for five years) is a valid signal not to weed.

While not as detailed as one might wish, the report is really one of the most important available on the subject of weeding. It stresses one of the most troublesome problems faced by weeders—i.e., the problem that occurs when faculty and staff encounter such negative words and phrases as "selective book retirement program," "seldom-used scholarly books," "storage," "discarding," and "obsolescence."[12] Overcoming the emotional response to what should be an objective procedure remains an unsolved problem.

In another direction, Ash approached the problem of the impact of storage on the overall use of the collection. He reported that in two years only 3-1/3 percent of the library usage came from the stored collection. Therefore:

> . . . the use of storage books at Yale is so limited that problems are not likely to occur in library service.[13]

A reasonably large part of this study dealt with various aspects of compact storage and the advantages of the Yale system. He included detailed cost data, and one of the major factors influencing the costs:

> Four and one half times as many books can be shelved by the Yale Compact Storage Plan as in conventional stack arrangement.[14]

He also reported a cost of storage at $0.61 per volume. This section of the work is invaluable for anyone considering compact storage, especially if it is studied along with Ellsworth's fine book.[15]

For the more conventional weeders, Ash offered strong support:

> In the actual process of selection for a book retirement program, we have found very little that can be reduced to a formula or routine.

> . . . the execution of selective book retirement becomes increasingly a matter of knowledge, judgment and wisdom.

> [Weeding] cannot be determined solely on the basis of use.[16]

4. **Mueller, Elizabeth.** One of Mueller's substantial contributions was the identification of the characteristic that makes the age of a volume a poor predictor of future use.[17] Although more new titles were reported in circulation than older ones, on the average, in several cases she reported that certain older titles had circulation characteristics very similar to those of the new titles. This study, made in six public libraries, was an attempt to compare the non-fiction circulation characteristics of new versus old titles.

She also reported on fiction circulation rates. Her rates of 4.4 to 7.3 circulations per volume per year can be compared to 2.8 to 6.2 volumes in this author's *Five Library Study*. Neither the size of the population nor the size of the collection correlates with this circulation characteristic.

5. **Buckland, M. K.** In a broader study at the University of Lancaster in England, it was suggested that libraries attempt to uncover ". . . objective information about the best ways of providing a library service in a university."[18]

> [Traditional techniques] do not tell one how many books to buy, *how long to keep them* [italics mine], or how long the loan period should be.[19]

This study was an attempt to create computer-compatible mathematical models. Bradford's Law of Scattering[20] encouraged such an approach. One objective of Buckland's study was to determine "for how long should the documents, so painstakingly added to stock, be retained?"[21] It:

> . . . showed that, in a petroleum library which can accommodate about 2,000 volumes, about 190 titles all retained for about 11 years would constitute the most useful stock pattern and would satisfy about 75% of the requests.[22]

Using a mathematical formula for evidence, Buckland concluded:

> . . . effective is the policy of retaining heavily-used titles for a longer period than less heavily-used ones. In fact, as the usage of each volume declines with time there comes a point at which it would be cheaper to satisfy by interlibrary loan such requests as still occur rather than continue to incur storage costs.[23]

One of the assumptions of his formula—that the cost of discarding material is "trivial"—is a subject that needs considerably more study, as it has rarely been tested in a careful manner.

> . . . in practice this might not be true, and the situation could arise where it is cheaper *not* to discard even if a document is totally unused.[24]

Then, turning to the subject of core collections, Buckland reported what is a rather well-known characteristic of libraries—that ". . . 20% of the Lancaster stock generates 80% of borrowing."[25]

In this report, Buckland recognized the weakness of subjective weeding:

> It has been established that records of past use are the simplest and best available predictors of future use (considerably better than the unaided subjective judgment of either teachers or librarians); . . .[26]

6. **Morse, Philip.** In his recent book,[27] Morse has evaluated and reported on some of the findings of various studies made at M.I.T. He offered a series of concepts that he considered valuable for a discussion of the whole field of discarding books. He begins with a deceptively simple statement:

> . . . the librarian should know, as accurately as possible, what now is going on and should be able to predict what probably will be going on in the future.[28]

This is the whole thesis of Morse's approach to weeding—the predictability of future usage. Morse wanted to discover the "pattern" of book use; he said that data necessary for such information could be obtained. Since it is expensive to obtain, however, it has not been done. In business, where such data becomes essential for decision-making, it is acquired. He noted that computer use would make it easier to gather such data.[29]

As with most of the practical research on weeding, he noted that one of the great unsolved problems of weeding has been:

> . . . the traumatic one of destroying or otherwise getting rid of some of the less useful books, or the less drastic one of retiring some books to stacks or to deposit libraries, . . .[30]

Nevertheless, he recognized the need for a solution and suggested that:

> . . . it is important to be able to predict the future circulation of a book. . . . If one could retire only those books that had a chance of less than 1 in 6 or 1 in 10 of being asked for in the next year, the fraction of disadvantaged borrowers might be small enough to be endurable.[31]

Like most serious students of the subject, Morse reported that merely noting the age of a book does not take into consideration important use patterns displayed at M.I.T. He made the following statement:

> Thus, the conclusion that our year-by-year analysis led us, that the circulation behavior of a book depends (on an average) on its previous-year's circulation and not explicitly on its age or still earlier circulation, . . .[32]

He pointed out that it would be advantageous to discover what data is needed for decision-making in weeding. He also reported on a study of book retirement based upon the criteria of age and non-circulation. By non-circulation, he refers to volumes with relatively long shelf-time periods. Using age as a criterion caused 5,200 inconveniences, while using non-circulation as a criterion caused only 3,600 inconveniences.[33]

> . . . the [non-circulators] will circulate less often than the rest of the old books.[34]

7. **Slote, Stanley J**. This author[35] has conducted a use study involving non-book material. In most newspapers, metal "cuts" are used to produce the photographs that appear in print. These cuts are filed for reuse in case a person or event becomes newsworthy again. A systematic sample was taken from the entire collection. The conclusion was that no cut should be reused after the eighth year from its first use, provided that it had not been reused before. This meant that a shelf-time period of eight years would describe a core collection including all the cuts likely to be used in the future, provided that these cuts had been previously used only once.

It was also found that no cut had been used after its fourteenth year in the file, even if reused in the interim period. Ninety-two percent of the cuts had never been reused, an indication that better keeping criteria and procedures might have been called for. Thus, the age of the cut and/or the time between uses (shelf-time period) were combined to create the weeding criteria. Employing these criteria, 85 percent of the collection was weeded out.

This basic study alerted the author to the value of determining the "time between uses" (later called "shelf-time period"), which became the backbone of the present study. This study was an example of the practical use of objective data for weeding.[36]

8. **Grieder, Elmer**. Grieder was one of the first to point out the value of being able to *predict* the impact of secondary storage on service to the client.[37] He sought to find out how many volumes might be stored without "serious detriment to service." He made some statistical counts similar to those suggested in this volume, first recording the "date of last circulation" of books at the circulation desk. He tabulated this data from the charge slips representing volumes in circulation,[38] then sampled the books on the shelves for the same variable. This information was then tabulated, as shown in Table 3.

His conclusion was that 39.2 percent of the books had not circulated in the previous 15 years and thus 76,656 volumes could have been stored in secondary areas "with no serious disruption of service." He stated that he could predict the amount of future use of volumes to be stored.

To validate this belief, he made a two-week study of the books circulating, to determine the date-of-last-circulation. He reported that if these 15-year non-circulations had been stored, only 4.01 percent of the circulating volumes would have had to come from storage. If the 56,375 volumes that had not circulated in 20 years had been stored, only 2 percent would have had to come

Table 3

GRIEDER STUDY*, 1949

STANFORD UNIVERSITY LIBRARY
SHELF-TIME PERIODS OF THE CIRCULATION AND COLLECTION
SAMPLES COMPARED (%)

Cumulative Shelf-Time Period		
Date of Last Circulation	Collection	Circulation
1949	22%	63%
1948	32	79
1947	39	85
1946	44	87
1945	47	88
1940-1944	61	93
1935-1939	71	96
1930-1934	78	98
1925-1929	83	99
1920-1924	88	
1915-1919	92	
1910-1914	95	
1905-1909	98	
1900-1904	99	
Before 1899	100	100

*Figures revised and simplified.

from storage. This study is important in that it anticipated the conclusions made by later studies and uncovered the best techniques for the prediction of future demand.

9. **Cooper, Marianne**. This study reported on the practical application of objective and subjective weeding criteria.[39] After a rather thorough report on many of the previous studies in the area of weeding, Cooper reported on the application of Trueswell's approach (see page 67) to the collection at the Chemistry Library at Columbia in 1965.

The purpose of the study was to find a way to reduce the number of volumes on the accessible shelves in the library. The methodology was to observe 135 charge-out cards, and to tabulate the use patterns. The data presented was as follows:

99 percent had been borrowed at least once in the past 8 years.
97 percent had been borrowed at least once in the past 5 years.
95 percent had been borrowed at least once in the past 3 years.
71 percent had been borrowed at least once in the past 1 year.[40]

It was decided to keep in the active collection those borrowed at least once in the last five years and to transfer or store the rest. The faculty rechecked weeded volumes and returned to the active collection a number of the volumes selected. Thus, shelf-time period was not the sole criterion used for weeding; such criteria as reference value were also considered. This refusal to accept completely the objective criterion for weeding is not unusual.

10. **Houser, Lloyd J.** Much has been written about the age of volumes and the use of this element for identifying core collections. In 1944, Gosnell[41] produced the first serious study of this type for a university library.

A pilot study by Houser, [42] while not dealing with weeding, suggested that the reference collections of two public libraries might be evaluated by using the latest copyright date as well as by comparing their volumes with standard check lists. The Plainfield, N.J., Public Library and the Woodbridge, N.J., Public Library were the sample libraries.

He demonstrated the wide variation between the holdings in these two libraries and implied that the library with the more recent date-distribution might better serve its users. He mentioned four objections to the use of the date-distribution:

> a. The nature of publishing is such that a new copyright date does not necessarily mean that the information in the latest edition of a book title is quantitatively or qualitatively better than an earlier edition of the same title . . . [in fact there may be] . . . no change in the content of the original book.

> b. A number of titles remain standard works or are classics. . . .

> c. Some . . . works with earlier copyright dates may very well serve as adequately as similar works with later copyright dates.

> d. . . . an older edition of a work . . . may preclude the necessity of replacing it with its newer edition.[43]

Thus, this study highlighted some of the problems involved in using the imprint date as a weeding criterion.

Research Studies.

The remaining reports are all serious research efforts that relate directly to weeding criteria and that deal with the variables of age of the volume, shelf-time period, or both. Purposes, methodology, data, and findings are reported in detail. In most cases, they are doctoral dissertations, funded research projects, or shorter reports on such projects. They are considered to be most significant.

1. **Lister, Winston C.** Lister's dissertation[44] is an interesting example of library research with a goal of practical application. It focused on uncovering the real costs involved in compact storage in order to determine whether such storage should or should not be used.

Accepting the findings that the two best predictors of future usage are the age of the materials and the book usage rate, it studied the economic impact that results when these two criteria are used to select books for compact storage.

The study, which deals with academic libraries, expresses the opinion that removal of materials from the working collection is a solution to the ever-growing university library. Such storing is of value to the patrons, since they are then " . . . able to locate the bulk of their desired materials more easily and more quickly."[45] The study also attempted to uncover " . . . some way of determining the optimal number of books which should be separated into storage."[46]

The Lister study, at three Purdue University branch libraries, consisted of taking a 20 percent sample of the titles from the shelf list and tabulating use and age data by computer. A series of judgments were made concerning the costs of the various aspects of use and storage. These included building and equipment costs, maintenance and operating costs, circulation costs, and relocation costs. Formulas were developed to measure the total cost of using both criteria for decision-making. Since cost was the principle focus, weeding criteria were relegated to a rather junior position in this study.

The following conclusions are important:

> . . . the author sincerely believes that selection of an item for storage should be based entirely upon its current (or immediate past) rate of usage. . . . As has been repeatedly pointed out in the literature, other measures of usage are not nearly so reliable as past history. In this research the age criterion, which is apparently the next best predictor of usage, was found to be far inferior to the usage rate criterion for scientific monographs.[47]

> . . . there is evidence which illustrates extreme variability in the current usage rates of books of a common age, demonstrating the infeasibility of a single age-related obsolescence function. . .[48]

In addition, Lister affirmed two other points:

> It is possible to establish simple decision rules regarding the selection of library material for storage . . .[49]

> Intellectual weeding policies, which require judgment and are based upon somewhat intangible variables, usually turn out to be time consuming, expensive, and qualitative attempts to predict future usage.[50]

Of particular interest is Lister's explanation of why the age criterion is faulty.

> The age model is based upon the average behavior of obsolescence with age. . . . The variability about the average rate of usage for each age group is completely ignored. It is because this dispersion about the mean is often very significant that causes some authors to protest a storage decision rule predicated upon the ages of books and to support the usage rate criterion.[51]

Concluding that some mechanical techniques could be very helpful, he maintained that computerized circulation systems would make the whole weeding process much easier, from the point of view of both selecting the volumes to be removed and altering the catalogs to reflect such moves.[52] As an alternative, he suggested that:

> It might become advantageous to mark, in some way, the outside covers of the books to provide usage rate indicators.[53]

2. **Silver, Edward A.** Silver's study[54] was part of a series of reports emanating from an operations research course at Massachusetts Institute of Technology. He pointed out the space problem facing the library:

> . . . extra shelf space is rapidly diminishing due to the acquisition of new books. A possible course of action to remedy the situation is the use of weeding, . . .[55]

His approach was to investigate the effects of various decision criteria. His objective was to find a cut-point (a specific last date on a book card) that would enable the librarian to keep the number of books on the shelves at the same level, whenever it is applied. For example, if he wanted to keep 5,000 volumes on the shelves, he would find the cut-point that would give him this result.

Approximately 100 samples were chosen from eight different subject areas in the science library at M.I.T. These areas were: general science, math, physics, chemistry, geology, biology, engineering, and miscellaneous. The method decided upon was a systematic sample. The related variable was the "shelf-time since last circulation."

Among his conclusions were:

a.   That the exclusive weeding policy should be based upon shelf-time since last use.

b.   ". . . that a criterion of this nature eliminates the need of technical aid in the weeding operation."[56]

c.   That there are substantial variations among the different subject groups, in relationship to the selected variable.

d.   That there is also a substantial variation from the mean within each group.

e.   That books that never circulate or that contain no circulation data are a serious problem to the researcher in use studies of this kind.

He concluded that a weeding policy ought to be based upon the need for shelf space.

3. **Jain, Aridaman K.** Jain has produced two works that relate to book usage: the first is based upon pilot studies[57] and the second, a much more complete study, follows the leads uncovered in the pilot.[58]

In his pilot study, an interesting question was asked: what data can a librarian use to reconstruct usage patterns when historical records are not available? Jain was trying to identify criteria useful in selecting books for storage.

His methodology was to take a systematic sample of parts of the collection, using the shelf-list for selecting the sample. All the titles in current use during a five-week period, both at home and in the library, were recorded. An attempt was made to use the following as variables: a) language; b) country of publication; c) year of publication, and d) the year of accession. The method of evaluating the data was called "relative usage." It relates the number of titles being used in any category to the total number of volumes in the collection in the same category.

Although tables representing the data, the categories, and the findings (relative usage) were presented, no firm conclusions were reported, except that the findings could be used to make decisions for storing books. This exploratory study was an attempt to test a proposed methodology and a special approach.

In his more complete study, Jain pushed rigorously into the areas that he first explored in his pilot. His purpose was to study criteria that might be useful in determining titles to be stored in secondary locations. With an emphasis on mathematical models, he examined all the previous work done and hoped to develop a better mathematical approach.

In this study he emphasized the importance of use studies. In support of this opinion he listed 631 works relating to book usage, discussing the more thorough and outstanding works.[59]

His approach consisted of reviewing the previous work done, stating the weaknesses of these studies, and, through mathematical computation, developing a study without the same weaknesses. He covered sixty-one pages with mathematical proofs, which are difficult to follow.

His findings were two-fold. First, he was rather critical of all the previous studies, and stated their shortcomings in detail. Second, he offered his own formula. This is the "relative usage" found in the first study. Based upon this new approach, he concluded:

> In spite of the recent tendencies to overemphasize usage histories, this study shows that age is a significant variable in studying usage of monographs. As pointed out in this study, there are several problems associated with the usage histories of monographs and it is hard to say how much reliance can be placed

on the usage histories under the current methods of record keeping. Also, while usage rates of individual monographs have considerable variation even over a short period of time, the usage rates of various age groups do not show any significant differences over time.[60]

The phrase "overemphasize usage history" was found in his conclusions with no evidence found in his report that usage history was, in fact, studied by him and found wanting. This is the only study of significance that preferred to use age rather than usage as the criterion for weeding decisions.

4. **Fussler, Herman H., and Simon, Julian L.** Perhaps the most thorough research done in the area of use patterns has been by Fussler and Simon.[61]

They noted that accumulative growth of collections causes serious space problems for many libraries. One approach to the problem is compact storage of books, storage which will not impede effective access to needed materials. A fundamental question they attempted to answer is:

Will any kind of statistical procedure predict with reasonable accuracy the frequencies with which groups of books with defined characteristics are likely to be used in a research library?[62]

In order to select books for compact storage, this study endeavored to find a characteristic or variable that would predict which books were most likely and which least likely to be used.

The basic technique of the Fussler and Simon study was a modification (cross-sectional approach) of the historical approach to the past-use of individual books.[63] The data came from the entire collection, as compared to the "current circulation method," in which the data came from the circulation desk only. The historical method ideally consists of recording the complete history of the past uses of the volumes, and ranking all of the volumes in accordance with the number of such uses per year. Since not all data were available, the authors modified this and used the "cross-sectional approach," recording all uses during previously determined periods of time, five years and twenty years. They assumed that future usage would continue at the same rate as in the past (though slightly reduced). They then related this use-ranking to the variables to be considered, such as age of the volume or date of last use. How "good" the function was, was judged in relationship to a book storage program. The "best function" is the one that identifies the fewest books in a core collection, which would maintain a predetermined level of use. In other words, the "best function" permits the storing of the most books at a given use level.

Several variables or functions have been studied. These include the following, either alone or combined:

a.   publication date
b.   accession date
c.   language
d.   use in last five years
e.   years since last use

The study was further divided into three sections:

a.   Functions for libraries with no records of prior use.
b.   Functions that require five year past due records.
c.   Functions employing long records of past use.

A number of the conclusions in Fussler's study did not relate either to shelf-time period or to the age of a volume. The major findings that relate to these two variables are as follows:

> It becomes evident that books can be separated into groups that will generate significantly different amounts of use. Because of the differences between the patterns of holdings in various matters and in various libraries, the effects of any given rule cannot be predicted without knowing more about the subject area and the library. But an inexpensive and quick set of surveys should in most cases provide all the information necessary for applying the rules successfully.[64]

> . . . employing *years since last use* as the only variable, gives strikingly good results.[65]

> . . . characteristics such as the age of a book and its language are less satisfactory in predicting future use than is past use. It is doubtful that any other variable will suddenly appear on the research scene and greatly increase predictive accuracy.[66]

> *Past use, where sufficient data are available, was found to be the best single predictor of the future use of a book.*[67]

> The variable of past use is sufficiently powerful that for libraries with 20-year use records the objective characteristics make little further contribution.[68]

Using the historical method, Fussler and Simon did get better results when a longer use history was projected. They implied that differences in libraries necessitate individual study for each collection,[69] and they attempted to combine variables to see if a better criterion would result:

> Even if we consider the best of the rules that do not employ past use . . . the results are not very satisfactory.[70]

Fussler and Simon also approached the question of whether there are better ways to select books for storage. They compared their criteria with the results obtained from the consensus of a group of scholars in a subject field. Without rejecting the validity of scholars' judgment, they concluded:

The various parts of the investigation convince us that with our rules we may predict the future use of books at least as well as any other method known to us.

The objective system seems to agree with the consensus of a group of scholars . . .[71]

In one sense, Fussler and Simon's entire study was a validation. A prediction was made based on the use patterns prior to 1954, and the period of 1954 to 1958 was then checked to validate the prediction.

5. **Trueswell, Richard William.** Richard Trueswell has probably produced the most significant usage studies relating to the present work. Along with Fussler and Simon, he has established the basic framework of the study; Trueswell has published five works[72] that are significant.

In his dissertation,[73] Trueswell approached the weeding problem from the point of view of its applicability to data processing and computer techniques. The study consisted basically of a number of questionnaires used to determine the "behavioral patterns and requirements of users of a large university library system."[74] As a reinforcing effort, "samples of current circulation were made to determine circulation rates, charge date distributions, and book age distributions."[75] It was this offshoot of the main research that was of most interest.

The basic purpose of this part of the study was to identify a core collection. It was an assumption of Trueswell, gathered from the literature, that "only a very small portion of the library's holdings are in circulation very frequently."[76] He described this sub-set of volumes as the "core" and defined the term "core collection" as a percentage of the collection that should satisfy a given level of the user circulation requirements.[77]

His methodology was to examine the books currently circulating and to analyze them in terms of two variables: ". . . one in terms of book age and one in terms of the previous time that the book had been in circulation."[78] Concerning the present circulation, he maintained that it is reasonable to assume that the ". . . frequency distribution of the circulation is representative of future circulation. . . ."[79]

Another facet of Trueswell's discussion was determining an acceptable percentage for the circulation need unsatisfied by a core collection.[80] He suggested that perhaps 1 percent or less would be a desirable figure. His methodology attempted to create core collections at this level. His major findings were:

. . . approximately one-fourth of the current holdings in the Technical Institute Library should satisfy over 99 percent of the requirements for circulation.[81]

and that at Deering:

> ... 20% of the present holding could be expected to satisfy over 99% of the circulation requirements.[82]

Further, that:

> The core collection concept can be extended further for use as a tool to thin out the current holdings of the library. Analysis of circulation patterns reveal that over 99% of the current circulation activity is from a population of books each of which has been loaned at least once during the past 18 years for the Deering Library and the past 8 years for the Tech Library.[83]

In his second work,[84] Trueswell dealt with a strategy for weeding employing user needs as a criterion. Again he used "last circulation date" as a circulation predictor.

He began by stating that he did not advocate "the arbitrary thinning and discarding of books from a library" and that the decision to do so is a policy decision that must be made by the administration of the library.

Nevertheless, a major problem of libraries is how to cope with the increasing size of their holdings. Because periodicals are not very likely targets for thinning, the focus was on monographs. Among his conclusions were the following:

> It is suggested that the criteria for stack thinning should be designed to help the library satisfy the requirements of the users of the library.[85]

> This statistic, [age of the volume] when translated into the percentage of holdings satisfying a given percentage of circulation does not lead itself to thinning of monographs.[86]

Also of relevance was his clear-cut explanation of "cut-off date":

> We now have a way to remove books from the stacks by using the following decision rule: Remove all books that have not circulated during the previous eight year period.[87]

In Trueswell's next significant contribution,[88] he combined most of the information and opinion found in his two previous works, using the article to restate and reaffirm his findings. Here has been found the strongest statement as to the meaning of his findings.

> With this approach we are in effect saying that there is a predictable optimal number of volumes for a library's core collection that will satisfy a given percent of user circulation requirements.[89]

It appears that the last circulation date may be an ideal statistic to define and measure circulation requirements and patterns.[90]

It is possible that the last circulation date statistic could serve as a tool or a guide to assist the librarian in the stack thinning or weeding process.[91]

A rather general assumption made in this approach is that the circulation pattern as measured today is typical of the circulation pattern of five, ten, or twelve years in the past. This may not be an unreasonable assumption based on the original and subsequent data.[92]

In another article by Trueswell,[93] some new data were presented. The author studied two libraries not previously reported upon. These were the Mount Holyoke College Library and the Goodell Library, University of Massachusetts. The data from these libraries were compared with the Deering Library data. His conclusions were that "the experience of these three libraries proved to be surprisingly similar."[94]

He also suggested, for the first time, that this technique should have application in "circulation-oriented public libraries."[95]

His fresh approach toward identifying a core collection might have some practical use for libraries without adequate circulation records.

We, therefore, go back x years and starting at that point in time, we adopt in our model the procedure of placing a red X on the cover of each book borrowed. As time progresses, more and more of the books borrowed will have a red X on the cover. After several years, we will reach a point where ninety-nine percent of the books brought to the desk for circulation will already have red X's.[96]

At this point, the core collection would consist of all having the red X.

Trueswell's last work[97] was more detailed than his earlier journal articles. In it he recommended the employment of:

... the last circulation date as a statistic to help describe library user circulation requirements.[98]

This would determine what to hold and what to weed. He reported, in greater detail, on the same libraries dealt with before—Mount Holyoke, Goodell, and Forbes (Public) Library. He added a warning that:

It is extremely important that circulation systems incorporate procedures that will record in some way the date [of the circulations] ...[99]

He recommended that a further use of this data could help decide which titles should be acquired in multiple copies. While no clear-cut decision rule was given, it was suggested that volumes having the most recent circulation dates be considered first when ordering duplicating copies.

In an expanded approach, he emphasized that this method of tallying cumulative distribution functions of last circulation dates gives one a simple decision role that "allows a quantitative approach to an otherwise subjectively treated phenomena."[100] As such, it not only helps identify candidates for weeding, but it predicts the actual size of the core collection and the effect that weeding will have on future circulation. He again stated that:

> ... there is a group of books that could be called a core collection that circulates quite frequently and that only a very small percentage of circulation represents books that have not circulated within a relatively short time period.[101]

REFERENCES

1. Aridaman K. Jain and others, "A Statistical Study of Book Use Supplemented with a Bibliography of Library Use Studies" (unpublished Ph.D. dissertation, Purdue University, 1967).

2. Charles H. Busha and Royal Purcell, "A Textural Approach for Promoting Rigorous Research in Librarianship," *Journal of Education for Librarianship* XIV (Summer 1973), p. 3.

3. Charles William Eliot, "The Division of a Library Into Books in Use, and Books Not in Use, with Different Storage Methods for the Two Classes of Books," *Library Journal* XXVII (July 1902), pp. 51-56.

4. Ibid., p. 52.

5. Ibid.

6. Ibid.

7. Samuel H. Ranck, "The Problem of the Unused Book," *Library Journal* XXXVI (August 1911), pp. 428-29.

8. Ibid., p. 428.

9. Ibid., p. 429.

10. Lee Ash, *Yale's Selective Book Retirement Program* (Hamden, Conn.: Archon Books, 1963).

11. Ibid., p. 81.

12. Ibid., p. X.

13. Ibid., p. 28.

14. Ibid., p. 52.

15. Ralph E. Ellsworth, *The Economics of Book Storage in College and University Libraries* (Washington: Association of Research, 1969).

16. Ash, *Yale's Selective Book Retirement Program*, pp. 66-67.

17. Elizabeth Mueller, "Are New Books Read More Than Old Ones?" *Library Quarterly* XXXV (July 1965), pp. 166-72.

18. M. K. Buckland and others, *Systems Analysis of a University Library* (Lancaster: University of Lancaster Library Occasional Papers No. 4, 1970), p. 1.

19. Ibid.

20. S. C. Bradford, "Sources of Information of Specific Subjects," *Engineering* CXXXVII (January 26, 1934), pp. 85-86.

21. Buckland, *Systems Analysis of a University Library*, p. 8.

22. Ibid., p. 10.

23. Ibid., p. 12.

24. Ibid.

25. Ibid., p. 52.

26. Ibid., p. 53.

27. Philip M. Morse, *Library Effectiveness: A Systems Approach* (Cambridge, Mass.: M.I.T. Press, 1968).

28. Ibid., p. 1.

29. Ibid., p. 5.

30. Ibid., p. 83.

31. Ibid., pp. 83-84.

32. Ibid., p. 93.

33. Ibid., pp. 167-68.

34. Ibid., p. 168.

35. Stanley J. Slote, "An Approach to Weeding Criteria for Newspaper Libraries," *American Documentation* XIX (April 1968), pp. 168-72.

36. In the *Five Libraries Study*, much material was excluded from the sample because no data was available on the book card. It was felt that often this was because the material had never been used. Such observation led to the suggestion that all book cards be *dated* when placed into books.

37. Elmer M. Greider, "The Effect of Book Storage on Circulation Service," *College and Research Libraries* XI (October 1950), pp. 374-76.

38. This technique may have the weakness that books in the hands of the clients at any one moment may not represent the true circulation pattern. Certain types of books may be returned more rapidly than others, and then recirculated. For instance, if 1,000 fiction volumes and 1,000 non-fiction were in circulation at one time, and fiction was kept out for 10 days on an average while non-fiction was retained for 20 days, fiction would be under-represented by 50 percent in the sample.

39. Marianne Cooper, "Criteria for Weeding of Collections," *Library Resources and Technical Services* XII (Summer 1968), pp. 339-51.

40. Ibid., p. 349.

41. Charles F. Gosnell, "Obsolescence of Books in College Libraries," *College and Research Libraries* V (March 1944), pp. 115-25.

42. Lloyd J. Houser, *New Jersey Area Libraries: A Pilot Project Toward the Evaluation of the Reference Collection* (New Brunswick, N.J.: New Jersey Library Association, 1968).

43. Ibid., pp. 30-31. In this quotation, there have been omitted some of the specific references to the type of collection and volumes Houser was studying in order to relate these statements more closely to the present study.

44. Winston Charles Lister, "Least Cost Decision Rules for the Selection of Library Materials for Compact Storage" (unpublished Ph.D. dissertation, Purdue University, 1967).

45. Ibid., p. 12.

46. Ibid., p. 6.

47. Ibid., p. 223.

48. Ibid., p. 226.

49. Ibid., 224.

50. Ibid., p. 223.

51. Ibid., p. 103.

52. Ibid., p. 116.

53. Ibid., p. 115.

54. Edward A. Silver, "A Quantitative Appraisal of the M.I.T. Science Library Mezzanine with an Application to the Problem of Limited Shelf Space" (unpublished term paper for M.I.T. graduate course 8:75, Operations Research, 1962).

55. Ibid., p. 2.

56. Ibid., p. 50.

57. A. K. Jain, "Sampling and Short-Period Usage in the Purdue Library," *College and Research Libraries* XXVII (May 1966), pp. 211-18.

58. Jain, "A Statistical Study of Book Use."

59. Ibid., pp. 128-220.

60. Ibid., p. 125.

61. Herman H. Fussler and Julian L. Simon, *Patterns in the Use of Books in Large Research Libraries* (Chicago: University of Chicago Press, 1969).

62. Ibid., p. 2.

63. Ibid., p. 7.

64. Ibid., pp. 45, 52.

65. Ibid., p. 30.

66. Ibid., p. 31.

67. Ibid., p. 15.

68. Ibid., p. 144.

69. Ibid., pp. 66-67.

70. Ibid., p. 143.

71. Ibid., p. 147.

72. See bibliography for full citations of the five works.

73. Richard William Trueswell, "User Behavioral Patterns and Requirements and Their Effect on the Possible Applications of Data Processing and Computer Techniques in a University Library" (unpublished Ph.D. dissertation, Northwestern University, 1964).

74. Ibid., p. IV.

75. Ibid.

76. Ibid., p. 35.

77. Ibid., pp. 109-116.

78. Ibid., p. 44.

79. Ibid., p. 105.

80.   Ibid., p. 112.
81.   Ibid., p. 113.
82.   Ibid.
83.   Ibid., p. 180.
84.   Richard W. Trueswell, "A Quantitative Measure of User Circulation Requirements and Its Possible Effect on Stack Thinning and Multiple Copy Determination," *American Documentation* XVI (January 1965), pp. 20-25.
85.   Ibid., p. 22.
86.   Ibid.
87.   Ibid.
88.   Richard W. Trueswell, "Determining the Optimal Number of Volumes for a Library's Core Collection," *Libri* XVI (1966), pp. 49-60.
89.   Ibid., p. 58.
90.   Ibid., p. 59.
91.   Ibid.
92.   Ibid., p. 57.
93.   Richard W. Trueswell, "User Circulation Satisfaction vs. Size of Holdings at Three Academic Libraries," *College and Research Libraries* XXX (May 1969), pp. 204-213.
94.   Ibid., p. 204.
95.   Trueswell, "Determining the Optimal Number of Volumes for a Library's Core Collection," p. 49.
96.   Ibid., p. 52.
97.   Richard W. Trueswell, *Analysis of Library User Circulation Requirements* (Amherst: University of Massachusetts, 1968).
98.   Ibid., abstract.
99.   Ibid., pp. 2-3.
100.   Ibid., p. 22.
101.   Ibid., p. 7.

CHAPTER 9

THE RESEARCH STUDIES—ASSUMPTIONS

INTRODUCTION

Before embarking upon these research projects, the author accepted a number of assumptions, based on a thorough study of the literature and a series of exploratory studies. The acceptance of these assumptions formed the foundation of this work.

ASSUMPTIONS

A valid way to determine the value to society of a book in a library is by the use made of that book. The contention is that if a library book is *never used* it has no value to a library or to society. Based, in part, on Ranganathan's classical conclusion that "books are for use," the underlying idea is that libraries are social institutions created to fulfill some needs. Those who believe that preservation in itself is the main goal of all libraries will find this book to have little relevance.

Alternatively, *considerable* utilization of a library book is an important determinant of its value to society. While the quality of the purpose of the use may vary, some use is elementary in giving any value to a work. No claim has been made that a direct mathematical relationship exists—that the greater the number of uses the more value a book has to society. It has been claimed, rather, that absolute non-use of a work makes it of no value to a collection, and that substantial use is meaningful.

What is unlikely to be used should be removed from the primary collection areas of a library. It has been assumed that the removal of unused books from primary storage areas "improves" a library. How much material should be removed depends on the objectives of each library and how much inconvenience to patrons will occur if a rarely used work loses some of its accessibility.

Removal of books from primary collection areas will improve accessibility to the collection and reduce overall costs. Though a user may occasionally have to spend extra time locating or waiting for the material that has been made less accessible by weeding, overall he will find things more quickly and surely in a properly weeded core collection. From the library's point of view, several factors contribute to the concept that weeding of collections will ultimately reduce costs. It must be acknowledged that initially there will be expenses before the savings can be realized. The costs involved in this method of weeding are incurred by:

1. The developing of cut-point and shelf-time period data.
2. The physical removal of the non-core works from primary collection areas to secondary storage areas.
3. Supplying the client with materials either not readily available because they were discarded or made less accessible because of secondary storage.
4. Changing catalogs and records as a result of weeding.

However, savings will be effected by disposing of quantities of superfluous materials; this will reduce the need for library building expansion with its accompanying costs in capital and human effort.

The assumption that reducing the size of collections makes the remaining works more accessible has many implications. A weeded library is improved in appearance and users will show greater interest in the books remaining on the shelves. Smaller collections result in smaller catalogs that are easier to use and more convenient to handle. Smaller but more heavily used collections put the used works physically closer together. And it is possible that weeding actually results in an increase in total circulation.

In summary, a weeded collection is more economical than a non-weeded collection.

Secondary or slower access to works which are important to a serious user will not prevent successful research work. Those serious researchers now using published works in a sophisticated manner will continue to ferret out the materials needed even if the works are less accessible. When books are not moved to secondary storage areas, researchers still will not find all their materials in one place. No library amasses the totality of all works produced. In addition, books in a collection may be out, on reserve, etc., so that access may be limited anyway. Interlibrary loan, in many respects equivalent to drawing works from secondary storage, already plays a role in the research process.

All of these characteristics have conditioned the modern researcher to accept reduced access to certain of the works he needs or wants. It has been assumed that acceptance of these conditions as they exist implies that the slight extension of such patterns would not have a serious negative impact on the research process.

Lower costs and/or higher levels of services are vital objectives for libraries. In this two-part assumption it is simply affirmed that society benefits when it gets more for its money. As a social institution, the library should consider identical service at lower costs a meaningful objective.

It is likely that if libraries really operated efficiently, they could reduce their costs substantially and still retain the same level of services. A study of library statistics has shown a wide range of costs for apparently similar libraries. Inefficiency seemed to be a major explanation for the range of costs.

While it is the basic assumption that lower costs are beneficial, it is strongly recommended that the savings effected should be converted into a higher level of service to society.

CHAPTER 10

SUMMARY OF THE FIVE LIBRARY STUDY

LIMITS OF THE STUDY

In 1969, a research project was undertaken in five public libraries: Briarcliff and Tarrytown in New York state, and Morristown, Trenton, and Newark in New Jersey. In order to contain the scope of the work, a number of limitations were accepted.

1. The study developed information for the "popular" adult fiction collections. No other type of material was studied. This limitation to fiction was based on the assumption that a study of fiction circulation will reflect almost all of its usage, since there is little in-library use of this type of material.

2. No attempt was made to study the value of weeding or to determine its real impact. An assumption was made that weeding would save shelf space, but whether or not it would improve the collection and increase usage was still to be determined.

3. No study was made of the best or the most economical ways to dispose of weeded volumes, nor was the effect of such weeding on the client studied. Other researchers have studied in depth the economics of secondary storage and retrieval of such works. This study made no judgments as to disposition of weeded volumes except that they should be removed from the primary collection area.

4. No attempt was made to validate the various library weeding standards. This was partly because the standards themselves were not in agreement (rarely do they reveal the data upon which they are based) and partly because the shelf-time period criterion seems to replace them in a very satisfactory way.

5. The field study was limited to selected libraries located in New York state and New Jersey. However, the studies in the literature have never indicated any geographic differences in use patterns.

6. Only standard book materials were studied, excluding such materials as fiction recordings, large-type volumes, films, etc. This simplified the experiment, and casual observation showed very little usage of non-book fiction materials in these libraries. Foreign language volumes were omitted because they were few in number, they were segregated from the regular collection, and they received relatively little use.

76

7. No attempt was made to evaluate the relative importance or characteristics of the usage.

8. The effect of duplicate copies was considered, since it had been noticed that identical copies of fiction books seemed to have roughly the same use pattern. Conversely, when titles were of different appearance or in different locations, vastly different patterns of use evolved. The techniques used in this study dealt with volumes, not titles, so these behavioral patterns had no significance. There have been serious studies on multiple copies (e.g., Buckland's study[1]), especially relating to how many copies of a title should be purchased.

9. The effects that seasonal use patterns might have on the results were not studied. In studies of the entire collection for an extended period, certain seasonal patterns would be reflected in the data. However, in these studies only a few days of consecutive circulation were observed.

These research efforts must be reviewed as exploratory since they did not have any network of accepted theory or knowledge as their base. Nevertheless, the techniques suggested still may be used as the best available tool for identifying core collections.

OBJECTIVES OF THE STUDY

To determine if certain variables could be utilized to create meaningful weeding criteria for adult fiction collections in public libraries. Two variables were observed, recorded, and evaluated. These variables were:

1. The time a book remained on the shelf between its two last uses or, if now in circulation, between its present use and the immediate previous use. This variable is called "shelf-time period." Certain artificial shelf-time periods were established, especially when dealing with books on the shelves. The "time since the last use" is a minimum or open-end, shelf-time period for a book now on the shelf. Any future circulation would give it a real shelf-time period longer than the period measured.

2. The age of a book, as indicated by the most recent date printed on the title page or its verso. This is called the "imprint date" or the "most recent imprint date."

To determine if the shelf-time period of a book is a better predictor of future use than the most recent imprint date. By "better" was meant that the criterion would yield a core collection containing fewer volumes and still satisfy a given level of future use.

This core collection concept was an essential feature of the entire study. The core is a sub-set of the holdings that can be identified with reasonable assurance as being able to fulfill a certain predetermined percentage (say 99 percent) of the future demand on the present collection. Idealized, the core collection would contain *only* those volumes that will circulate (or be used) in the future. This study was designed to see how close one can get to the ideal.

To develop a mathematical or visual model for the core collection of each library in the sample. It was hoped that some generalized approach could be uncovered that would help other libraries identify core collections.

To determine if the pattern of current use of books circulating was as valid a predictor of future use as are historic reconstructions of circulation over longer periods of time. The question here, raised by Herman Fussler,[2] was a serious one. Fussler has suggested that there was a considerable difference between the results that would be achieved from sampling the circulation for a few days or weeks as compared with results if circulation were observed for 5 or 20 years.

Circulation could be reconstructed for any number of years, provided that book cards indicating each circulation date had been retained for all circulating volumes in use during that period. However, even without such records, a considerable part of the circulation could be reconstructed from book cards currently available.

Fussler suggested that the only valid way to determine shelf-time periods was to reconstruct historically, for a long period of time, the circulation of a library. An objective of this study was to check this assumption and see if it had validity.

METHODOLOGY OF THE STUDY

The five public libraries selected all had adult fiction collections and all used book cards that recorded previous use. An attempt was made to find libraries that differed in several ways: in the size of the populations served, in the size of the collections, in the types of communities served, in the amounts of money budgeted for library purposed, and in the hours of service. For some of the major characteristics of the sample libraries, see Table 4.

For several days, the *circulating* books were studied and the observations were used to establish the present circulation pattern. The objective of this effort was to obtain samples of no fewer than 400 volumes. (For the exact data, see Table 5.) From this sample, data was computed showing the distribution of shelf-time periods and the latest imprint date. These distributions were utilized to predict the patterns of future use as they related to these two variables.

In addition, systematic samples likely to approximate random samples were made of the total fiction *collections*. The same information collected at circulation was now tabulated for the entire collection. These statistics were employed to predict the percentage of the present collection that would be represented in the new core collection.

The explanation of one of the studies (Table 1, p. 30) might help to clarify this part of the experiment. Looking at the column headed Briarcliff, it is seen that 72 percent of the volumes checked out on the days of the study had been previously checked out within the last 30 days. Thus, 72 percent of the volumes fell into the zero month shelf-time period. An additional 7 percent had been previously checked out in a period between 30 and 60 days before. Thus, for the zero and one month shelf-time periods, 79 percent of the volumes now being checked out had been checked out within the last 60 days.

Table 4

SELECTED CHARACTERISTICS OF THE FIVE SAMPLE LIBRARIES

Library	Population in Area Supporting Library	Number of Volumes Reported	Total Circulation	Dollars Spent	Number of Adult Fiction Circulations Last Year	Number of Adult Fiction Volumes	Number of Circulations Per Fiction Volume
Newark, N.J. Main Branch	405,220*	Est.** 1,000,000	1,377,389	$2,474,853**	46,349	31,356	1.5
Trenton, N.J. Main Branch	114,167*	218,370**	97,456	323,206	15,985	11,418	1.4
Morristown, N.J.	38,310	95,645	180,242	139,750	54,119	8,748	6.2
Tarrytown, N.Y.	19,880	44,036	95,948	100,533	33,988	12,420	2.8
Briarcliff Manor, N.Y.	5,714	14,450	35,293	27,544	12,399	3,520	3.5

*Served by more than this branch.
**In entire system.

Table 5

DATA RELATING TO SAMPLES TAKEN IN THE FIVE PUBLIC LIBRARIES

Source of Variable Sample	Briarcliff		Tarrytown		Morristown		Trenton		Newark	
					Number of Samples					
	Taken	Usable	Taken	Usable	Taken	Usable	Taken	Usable	Taken	Usable
Circulation--Shelf-Time Period	404	353	400	383	394	377	367	345	392	385
Circulation--Imprint Date	404	394	400	382	394	337	367	341	392	377

Collection Shelf-Time Period
  Sample 1
  Sample 2
	708
	352
	356
		668
		334
		334
			538
			270
			268
				475
				240
				235
					478
					243
					235
						427
						217
						210
							479
							253
							226
								464
								243
								221
									460
									234
									226
										439
										226
										213

Collection Sample--Imprint Date	708	694	538	530	478	444	479	461	460	444
Date on Which Collection Sample was Made	4/25/69		4/24/69		5/5/69		5/9/69		5/2/69	
Circulation Sample Consisted of All Volumes Borrowed for Following Number of Days	10		4		2		9		3	

Average Loan Periods For:
  1 week books
  2 week books
  3 week books
  4 week books
	8 days
	11 days
	19 days
			10 days
			20 days
					6 days
					19 days
							12 days
							26 days
									17 days (combined avg.)	

The next column yields similar information about the entire fiction collection—information obtained by systematically sampling the books on the shelves and all other books contained in the collection (such as the books in circulation). For Briarcliff it was found that the shelf-time variable was such that only 22 percent fell into the zero month shelf-time period and 30 percent into the zero and first month shelf-time period cumulatively.

This led to the conclusion that 30 percent of the collection would satisfy 79 percent of the present demand. The variable of shelf-time period can be used to describe books in a circulating library. If this present characteristic remains constant in the future, the past use pattern will accurately describe the future use.

In order to check upon the validity of the constancy of shelf-time period, another study was undertaken. A use-prediction was made for the Tarrytown library, based upon the shelf-time period variable. Seven weeks later, a new circulation sample was taken and compared with the prediction. Thus, a validation study was made.

THE DATA

In order to undertake the above studies, a series of decisions were made as to what data should be recorded. Although not all of this data was applied in each part of the study, it all had some relevancy. The following information was accumulated in the original study.

The last imprint data. This data was used to discover if the last imprint date was as good a predictor of future use as the last shelf-time period.

The three most recent due-dates on the book cards. This helped establish the shelf-time period for each volume in the collection, and was used for part of the study omitted from this book. It helped to recreate the historical patterns of use.

The number of circulations indicated for each of the last three years. This data helped reconstruct three years of use patterns, as part of the study of the historical reconstruction method for determining weeding criteria.

Notes. Special data was recorded relating to the loan period, membership in the McNaughton Collection,[3] lack of data, and any other information that seemed pertinent. It was used to compute shelf-time periods more accurately. It helped to reconstruct a three-year history of McNaughton Collection use—a special problem, since these books and their records were not parts of the permanent collection.

The sample sheets also showed the dates of the experiment, the sample source, and the sample method. (See Appendix B, page 143 for a sample page.)

MAJOR FINDINGS

1. Past use patterns are highly predictive of the future use of fiction volumes. The validation study corroborated this finding (see Table 6).

Table 6

VALIDATION STUDY—TARRYTOWN

THE PREDICTED CORE COLLECTION AND ITS
IMPACT ON FUTURE USE

	Predicted		Observed		If Weeded, Percent of Use That Would Have Been Retained
	In Core	Not In Core	In Core	Not In Core	
Number of books at 95% prediction level of future use (13 mo. and longer)	323	17	318	22	93.5
Number of books at 99.0% prediction level (38 mo. and longer)	337	3	338	2	99.4

2. The "shelf-time period" is a predictor of a "better" core collection than the "most recent imprint date," since it describes a smaller core collection for the same level of use. While it was found that imprint date *may* be a predictor of future use, it has little practical value. Using that criterion for weeding would automatically remove literary classics from the shelves.

3. An individual model (i.e., "an idealized standard for conparison" rather than a mathematical model) is required for each individual library. This model, which can be constructed from the circulation pattern, assumes that the "anticipated usage" is an acceptable standard for defining a core collection. Generalized shelf-time period criteria do not seem likely at this time. It is *possible* that, with certain other known variables (such as circulation per volume, number of volumes, number of new books added per year, etc.), generalized weeding criteria can be developed; such generalizations, however, are beyond the scope of this study.

4. The "current circulation" method creates use patterns that are as valid for predicting future use as is the method of "historical reconstruction." However, seasonal variations, although not studied in this experiment, became very apparent. In order to avoid serious error (due to seasonal usage), circulation patterns should be tested over a whole year.

5. The serious studies in this field, based on other types of collections, reinforced the major findings of this study. Almost all the other studies have dealt with academic libraries and have identified useful core collections.

Appendix A discusses these and other conclusions in greater detail and includes some of the supporting evidence. Of particular importance are the tables and figures that summarize the data collected and observed.

REFERENCES

1. M. K. Buckland and others, *Systems Analysis of a University Library* (Lancaster: University of Lancaster Library Occasional Papers No. 4, 1970).

2. Herman H. Fussler and Julian L. Simon, *Patterns in the Use of Books in Large Research Libraries* (Chicago: University of Chicago Press, 1969).

3. For an explanation of the McNaughton Collection, please refer to page 153 of Appendix B.

CHAPTER 11

SUMMARY OF THE STUDY OF THE
HARRISON PUBLIC LIBRARY

BACKGROUND

The study of the Harrison, N.Y., Public Library was undertaken for the purpose of putting into practical use the theoretical findings of the previous study. The Harrison library had outgrown its present facilities and was about to begin a traditional weeding program. The author was contacted, and he agreed to direct the weeding.

Before he began the weeding, he was given an opportunity to establish shelf-time information. It was agreed that not *all* candidates for weeding need be removed from primary collection areas. By leaving them in primary areas, the author tried to confirm the prediction that the non-core collection would have relatively little future use.

OBJECTIVES

To validate the theory of weeding by use of the shelf-time period criteria. This was the primary purpose of the study. The weeding criteria were to be established so that approximately 95 percent of the future use of the collection would be retained. Since the library was to be weeded by broad class (e.g., adult fiction or adult non-fiction), it could be observed whether the predicted amount of circulation was retained, as well as whether a weeded class retained its proportional share of the circulation.

To find out how classes of books varied in shelf-time period. Here an attempt was made to identify the largest library classifications that would be practical for establishing shelf-time periods. Previous research showed that different classes of materials had different shelf-time period characteristics, but such a study had never been reported for public libraries.

To validate a mechanical and simplified method of identifying the core collection, as suggested by Trueswell.[1] Here a library using the transaction card system was to identify its core through a system independent of the normal circulation records. Red dots were applied to the spine of all books charged out or added to the collection. When 95 percent of the books of a class being charged out at circulation had red dots, the core collection was identified as those books having red dots on the spine.

To uncover the practical problems involved in using the system described above. Both the human and the mechanical problems were studied.

To compare the shelf-time period data of the *Five Library Study* **with data from the Harrison Public Library**. To do this, considerable data was collected that had no relevance to the weeding procedure. For example, all red-dotted books in the collection were counted monthly, so that collection characteristics could be described.

THE LIBRARY

The Harrison Public Library serves a suburban New York City population of 22,000. The main library circulates over 120,000 volumes per year. With holdings of about 35,000 volumes, there is a yearly circulation rate of 3.4 uses per volume. The library is in a modern, cheerful buildings, and is extremely well-run.

THE METHODOLOGY

As in the previous study, information was sought about the characteristics of both the core collection, which passes through the circulation desk, and the non-core collection, which remains unused on the shelves. The circulation and acquisition departments were requested to apply a red dot on the lower two inches of the spine of each circulating volume. These dots, which were 1/4" in diameter, were self-sticking; their purpose was to indicate a shelf-time period, expressed in terms of either being "dotted" or "undotted." Thus, after ten months, all volumes with dots had circulated within the last ten months and therefore had a ten-month shelf-time period.

Every month a three-day count was taken at circulation of dotted and undotted books. When it was consistently observed that 95 percent of a class of books were dotted and circulating, that class could be weeded. The dotted books identified the core collection; the undotted, the weeded collection. In a normal weeding situation, this is the only part of the methodology that should be replicated.

Much more complicated was the study made of the collection. Here data was obtained for no practical weeding purpose, but only to enable a comparison between the statistics created in this and former studies. The following steps were taken:

1. Before the study started, the total collection was counted and categorized by class.

2. New volumes added to and removed from the collection were tabulated and used to determine the size of the collection.

3. Every month all red dotted books on the shelves were counted.

4. Each month all volumes in circulation were counted, their number estimated by class, and the totals added to the numbers found in Step 3.

5. The photo print-out of all circulating book cards was studied every three or four months to determine distribution of books in circulation by class.

All of the above data was tabulated and percentages were computed where relevant. (See Tables 7, 8, 9, 10, 11, and 12).

In addition, other useful data was accumulated. The number of books circulated per month, the number of books withdrawn, etc., were tabulated and used along with other relevant figures.

THE FINDINGS

The circulation of a weeded class was not affected seriously by weeding out substantial portions of the non-core collection. In fact, proportionately, fiction circulation increased 6.2 percent after 1,200 volumes were removed (see Table 10). In absolute numbers, fiction circulation increased after weeding, even though total adult circulation went down (see Table 11).

In another check during February 1974, fiction still represented 48.6 percent of the total circulation, an increase of 3.3 percent over its pre-weeded circulation. At the same time, biography was checked six weeks after a complete weeding and it still retained its 3.4 percent share of the total circulation.

This technique of weeding is much simpler and easier to use than other methods of weeding in current practice. However, the weeding process itself was delayed while data was being developed. For instance, it took seven months to develop the adult fiction weeding signal, and over fifteen months for the children's fiction signal.

Serious monthly pulsations of circulation patterns called for caution against making final decisions too rapidly. A pattern should be developed from a substantial sample (400+) so that sampling error does not distort the result. However, once a weeding signal is received the collection should be weeded immediately, so that non-core books do not appear in the core collection.

There are substantial differences in shelf-time periods among the various classes of books. In Harrison, eight such useful classes were identified. In *adult books*, the major classes are fiction (including short stories, science fiction, and mysteries), paperback, biography, and non-fiction; the *children's books* are divided into fiction, picture book, biography, and non-fiction. In this experiment, the differentiation of the non-fiction Dewey classes did not aid in making meaningful weeding decisions. The classes used most had very similar use patterns. The classes used least produced too few samples to create meaningful data and in any event their effect on the overall circulation was not significant.

There are a series of very practical, mechanical problems involved in the use of this system of creating shelf-time periods. A number of these concerned the red dot system. Due to the carelessness of circulation clerks, a number of

Table 7

SHELF-TIME PERIODS OF THE CIRCULATION AND COLLECTION SAMPLES COMPARED (%),
HARRISON, ADULT SECTION

Cumulative Shelf-Time Period	Fiction		Paperbacks		Biography		Non-Fiction 000–999+		Total	
	Circula-tion	Collec-tion	Circula-tion	Collec-tion	Circula-tion	Collec-tion	Circula-tion	Collec-tion	Circula-tion	Collec-tion
0	49	29	–	29	–	8	47	13	50	17
1	78	42	68	26	67	14	60	21	70	26
2	97	51	77	35	100	17	72	26	83	32
3	84	57	64	45	62	20	69	29	75	36
4	86	63	73	54	75	23	66	35	76	42
5	76	75	88	63	86	30	77	43	78	52
6	96	78	90	63	100	27	83	47	90	54
7	95	80	63	69	79	36	74	51	83	59
8	96	84	85	73	75	43	82	53	87	61
9	95	85	90	64	88	42	84	57	90	63
10	99*	93	77	68	81	44	77	59	86	69
11	99	93	87	71	92	46	93	61	96	73
12	98	93	84	69	90	42	89	60	94	72
13	99	95	91	74	91	61	92	69	96	80
14	98	–	80	–	91	–	90	–	93	–
15	99	–	91	–	91	–	90	–	94	–

*Collection weeded.

Table 8

SHELF-TIME PERIODS OF THE CIRCULATION AND COLLECTION SAMPLES COMPARED (%), HARRISON, CHILDREN'S SECTION

Cumulative Shelf-Time Period	Fiction		Picture Books		Biography		Non-Fiction		Total	
	Circulation	Collection	Circulation	Collection	Circulation	Collection	Circulation	Collection	Circulation	Collection
0	62	33	61	61	43	8	39	17	58	28
1	81	37	63	78	–	12	68	23	75	23
2	84	46	71	78	–	14	80	27	76	29
3	81	51	87	83	14	17	58	29	75	33
4	77	54	71	86	100	20	59	35	70	37
5	90	56	89	90	63	22	49	37	73	40
6	85	58	94	95	100	26	73	47	86	48
7	88	60	95	95	52	30	75	48	84	49
8	91	61	95	89	50	39	79	49	88	49
9	90	68	100	89	71	42	91	55	91	53
10	85	70	90	89	43	48	86	57	84	55
11	90	69	92	81	–	49	81	59	88	55
12	90	75	90	88	60	49	88	59	88	57
13	92	77	86	–	83	54	90	65	90	61
14	97	–	100	–	62	–	89	–	96	–
15	100	–	100	–	71	–	91	–	96	–

Table 9

SHELF-TIME PERIODS OF THE CIRCULATION AND COLLECTION SAMPLES COMPARED (%),
FIVE LIBRARIES AND HARRISON

Cumulative Shelf-Time Period (Mos.)	Briarcliff		Tarrytown		Morristown		Trenton		Newark		Harrison Adult Fiction	
	Circulation	Collection	Circulation	Collection	Circulation	Collection	Circulation	Collection	Circulation	Collection	Circulation	Collection
0	72	22	69	24	87	41	55	12	49	14	49	29
1	79	30	77	34	93	52	65	16	62	19	78	42
2	85	37	83	42	97	56	70	20	70	22	97	51
3	86	41	85	47	–	60	76	22	75	26	84	57
4	90	47	88	51	98	63	79	24	78	29	86	63
5	94	52	89	55	–	65	80	27	81	32	76	75
6	96	56	91	58	–	68	82	29	83	34	96	78
7	97	64	93	61	99	71	85	31	84	36	95	80
8	–	68	–	62	–	72	86	33	–	39	96	84
9	98	70	–	65	–	74	–	35	87	41	95	85
10	–	72	94	67	–	75	88	37	88	42	–	–
20	99	84	97	82	100	84	93	53	95	60	–	–
30	100	92	98	89	–	90	–	61	97	70	–	–
40	–	96	–	94	–	93	97	67	99	74	–	–
50	–	99	99	96	–	96	–	72	–	78	–	–
60	–	–	–	97	–	–	98	74	–	83	–	–
100	–	100	100	99	–	97	99	80	100	92	–	–
200	–	–	–	–	–	–	–	92	–	98	–	–
300	–	–	–	100	–	100	100	97	–	–	–	–
400	–	–	–	–	–	–	–	99	100	100	–	–
600	–	–	–	–	–	–	–	100	–	–	–	–

Table 10

THE IMPACT OF WEEDING ON CIRCULATION, HARRISON, ADULT FICTION

BEFORE WEEDING

	Total Circulation (in sample)	Fiction Circulation (in sample)	% of Total Circulation Represented by Fiction
Aug. 1972	320	172	
Sept.	176	72	
Oct.	641	281	
Nov.	610	279	
Dec.	620	291	
Jan. 1973	527	266	
Feb.	745	321	
Mar.	621	239	
Apr.	578	272	
Total	4,838	2,193	45.3

AFTER WEEDING

	Total Circulation (in sample)	Fiction Circulation (in sample)	% of Total Circulation Represented by Fiction
May 1973	724	291	
June	486	262	
July	837	470	
Aug.	572	332	
Sept.	573	301	
Oct.	842	423	
Total	4,034	2,079	51.5

Proportionate Increase of Fiction Circulation: 6.2%

Table 11

TOTAL ADULT FICTION CIRCULATION—BEFORE AND AFTER WEEDING—HARRISON

1973 vs. 1971

	Before Weeding 1971	After Weeding 1973	Increase in Total Number of Circulations After Weeding
May	2,598 volumes	2,600 volumes	
June	2,995	3,260	
July	3,309	3,480	
August	3,152	3,680	
September	2,731	3,020	
October	2,745	3,443	
November	2,446	3,153	
Total	19,976 volumes	22,636 volumes	2,660

1973 vs. 1972

	Before Weeding 1972	After Weeding 1973	Increase in Total Number of Circulations After Weeding
August	3,880 volumes	3,680 volumes	
September	2,820	3,020	
October	3,190	3,443	
November	3,180	3,153	
Total	13,070 volumes	13,296 volumes	226

Table 12

**PERCENTAGE OF USE VERSUS PERCENTAGE OF HOLDINGS,
HARRISON, ADULT COLLECTION**

Adult Collection

Class	Percentage of Circulation Represented by This Class	Percentage of the Library's Holdings Represented by This Class
Fiction	48.2	25.8
Paperbacks	6.5	3.0
Biography	3.4	5.5
Non-Fiction-Other	41.9	65.7
Total	100.0%	100.0%

Children's Collection

Class		
Fiction	45.5	40.1
Picture Books	25.8	11.9
Biography	2.6	5.2
Non-Fiction-Other	26.1	42.8
Total	100.0%	100.0%

books went through circulation undotted. This carelessness was countered by regular surprise inspections of this station for several months until dotting became routine. In addition, the clerks were given three independent opportunities to make sure that books were dotted: at check in, check out, and reshelving stations. Several orientation sessions were held with the clerks, at which times it was emphasized that if useful books got through undotted, the core collection might well be weeded instead of retained. In these ways, the dotting procedure was improved.

The mere fact that a dot was put on a book, however, did not ensure that it would become a permanent part of the book. Many dots fell off, and occasionally children pulled them off. To combat this, two dots were put on each volume (and often three on children's books) instead of one. Signs explaining the importance of the dots were placed around the library and closer supervision of book-handling (especially by children) was effected.

An unresolved problem was the identification of books receiving in-library use. No attempt was made to solve this problem. It is suggested that in future studies, all reshelving of books used in the library be done by clerks who will apply dots to the volumes before placing them on the shelves. While in-library use has been reported as being similar to circulating use, it is certainly not identical.

The usage patterns differed substantially from those developed in the earlier experiment (see Table 9). In the earlier experiment, since the dates on cards were used cumulatively, each successive shelf-time period showed a larger number. In practice, it may be found that fewer dotted books are used in one month, mainly because of seasonal fluctuations or special usage patterns (such as school assignments). The patterns developed were similar over a period of time (see Table 9). It is also possible that the variations were caused by sampling errors.

The library holdings are not in proportion to library usage. Although 25 percent of the Harrison holdings are adult fiction, over 48 percent of the usage was in fiction. On the other hand, 66 percent of the holdings are non-fiction, but only 42 percent of the usage (see Table 12). It is possible that the drop in fiction usage frequently noted in the literature has been caused by the acquisition policies of libraries.

Non-core volumes, retained because of professional judgment, should have been weeded. Some 400 non-core volumes were retained and were predicted to produce only 1 percent of the future circulation. In fact, they did represent between 1 percent and 2 percent of the circulation in each of the successive 6 months. This can be seen in Table 7, where the usage of the dotted volumes represented 98 to 99 percent of the total usage.

SUMMARY

This study added considerable practical information that will be helpful in weeding library collections. It is likely that further field experience will continue to add useful information.

REFERENCES

1. Richard W. Trueswell, "Determining the Optimal Number of Volumes for a Library's Core Collection," *Libri* XVI (1966), pp. 49-60.

CHAPTER 12

PATTERN OF USE IN LIBRARIES

GENERAL USE PATTERNS IN LIBRARIES

Many aspects of use patterns unfolded as the studied developed. Questions arose as to whether these patterns of use had changed over the years. Perhaps shelf-time periods had altered radically as new users patronized the library or new subject areas developed. A search of the literature was undertaken and wherever related data was discovered it was converted into data that could be compared with the original findings of these studies. It soon became apparent that there were great similarities between current and older use patterns. Tables 13 through 19 show some of the striking similarities.

In 1911, Ranck published some of his data. His report (Table 13), showing 84.9 percent of the fiction being charged out with a 24-month shelf-time period, is almost identical to the 85 percent found in the Tarrytown Public Library nearly sixty years later. As can be seen in the same table, Lister, studying research libraries and non-fiction, had patterns that closely resembled those of both the Trenton and the Newark Public Libraries.

As with all the data cited in these tables, there is a strong overall tendency for books to have high levels of use during the early shelf-time periods, and a much lower relative amount of use in later periods. However, it can be observed that in research collections, the shelf-time periods are much longer than in public libraries at identical use levels.

For example, Ranck reached the 85 percent usage level with volumes having a 24-month shelf-time period (Table 13). In Lister's study, this hovered around the 120-month shelf-time period. Silver reported M.I.T.'s geology collection at 58 percent for the 120-month shelf-time period, with a long way to go to reach 85 percent. Even Trenton was beyond 120 months, while Tarrytown reported the same circulation pattern occurring at 24 months. Large reference libraries, which tend not to weed their collections, have longer shelf-time periods than small public libraries serving a more recreational function. This is the striking characteristic demonstrated in all these tables.

One hypothesis is that the length of the shelf-time periods of circulating volumes relates to the average number of uses per volume in a collection. As this decreases, either because of the large number of volumes compared to the number of users in a library or because of a general public disinterest in a part of

94

Table 13

COMPARISON OF THE DATA

SLOTE VS. LISTER, RANCK, AND SILVER
SHELF-TIME PERIODS OF THE COLLECTIONS COMPARED
CUMULATIVE PERCENT OF THE COLLECTION CHARGED
OUT WITHIN THIS SHELF-TIME PERIOD

Shelf-Time Period in Months	24	60	120	Over 120
Ranck-Grand Rapids[1]				
Total Collection	79.2%	90.4%	95.8%	100.0%
Fiction Only	84.9	–	–	–
Lister-Purdue[2]				
Pharmacy	47.0	72.0	82.0	100.0
Physics	53.0	78.0	89.0	100.0
Chemistry	70.0	82.0	89.0	100.0
Silver-M.I.T.[3]				
Geology	19.2	43.7	58.2	100.0
General Science	20.2	49.3	69.4	100.0
Engineering	21.5	47.0	68.4	100.0
Biology	37.4	58.5	75.7	100.0
Miscellaneous	37.6	64.1	85.0	100.0
Mathematics	55.5	68.8	83.2	100.0
Chemistry	57.0	75.8	85.2	100.0
Physics	65.9	78.9	91.1	100.0
Slote-Five Public Libraries--Fiction				
Trenton	55.8	73.5	82.8	100.0
Newark	62.9	82.7	92.9	100.0
Tarrytown	85.0	96.8	98.9	100.0
Morristown	87.4	96.5	99.7	100.0
Briarcliff	87.9	99.7	100.0	–

Table 14

COMPARISON OF THE DATA

SLOTE VS. BLASINGAME
IMPRINT DATE CHARACTERISTICS OF THE COLLECTION
PERCENT OF BOOKS OF THIS AGE OR LESS
IN THE FICTION COLLECTION

Age in Years	Blasingame Library G[4]	Slote, Newark	Blasingame Library C[5]	Slote, Briarcliff
0–5	15%	14%	33%	30%
6–10	32	33	51	59
11–15	50	48	74	78
16–20	70	64	84	86
21–25	81	73	89	91
26–30	87	81	92	93
31–35	90	89	95	98
36–40	94	93	96	98
41–45	96	94	–	–
46–50	97	95	97	99
51–55	98	95	–	–
56–60	99	95	–	–
61–65	–	96	98	–
66 and over	100	100	100	100

Table 15

COMPARISON OF THE DATA

SLOTE VS. COOPER AND TRUESWELL
SHELF-TIME CHARACTERISTICS OF THE CIRCULATION
PERCENT OF THE SAMPLE NOT PREVIOUSLY
CHARGED OUT DURING THE CUMULATIVE TIME PERIOD

Shelf-Time Period (Mos.)	Cooper[6]	Trueswell[7]		Slote				
	Columbia	Tech	Deering	Morris-town	Briar-cliff	Tarry-town	Newark	Trenton
0	–	79%	89%	13%	28%	31%	51%	45%
1	–	49	76	7	21	23	38	35
2	–	42	68	3	15	17	30	30
3	–	34	59	2	14	15	25	24
4	–	26	51	–	10	12	22	21
5	–	25	49	1	6	11	20	20
6	–	23	42	–	5	9	17	18
12	29%	12	29	0	1	5	10	10
24	5	6	17	–	0	2	5	5
36	3	3	11	–	–	–	2	3
48	1	–	8	–	–	1	1	2
60	–	–	6	–	–	0	0	1

Table 16

COMPARISON OF THE DATA

SLOTE VS. TRUESWELL AND JAIN
IMPRINT AGE CHARACTERISTICS AT CIRCULATION
PERCENT OF THE CIRCULATION SAMPLE
Y YEARS OR LESS IN AGE

Age of Books in Years (Y)	Trueswell[8]		Jain[9]			Slote				
	Tech	Deering	Chemistry	Physics	Pharmacy	Briarcliff	Tarrytown	Morristown	Trenton	Newark
1*	17%	11%	8%	9%	8%	64%	47%	47%	33%	29%
2	29	16	21	18	19	68	50	60	41	39
3	35	23	31	28	26	71	54	66	46	47
4	44	26	41	38	32	73	58	69	52	51
5	50	30	48	44	37	76	61	72	56	58
6	55	33	54	53	43	78	63	74	60	61
7	59	38	59	57	50	80	66	78	65	66
8	62	43	63	61	55	83	72	82	70	71
9	64	47	68	65	60	84	75	84	73	74
10	66	50	72	68	63	85	78	86	76	77
11	70	52	75	71	66	86	81	88	79	81
20	-	-	93	87	88	96	93	93	92	94
30	-	-	97	93	95	99	97	96	97	99
over 30	100	100	100	100	100	100	100	100	100	100

*Includes books 16 months old or less, in some cases.

Table 17

COMPARISON OF THE DATA

SLOTE VS. JAIN
THE IMPACT ON CIRCULATION OF REMOVING VOLUMES
BASED ON IMPRINT AGE

Slote			Jain[10]		
Briarcliff			Purdue-Economics		
Year Cut-Point	Percent of Use Lost	Percent of Collection Weeded	Percent of Use Lost	Percent of Collection Weeded	Year Cut-Point
1946	3.8	9.7	4.3	10.0	1915
1954	8.4	19.1	8.6	20.0	1927
1958	13.5	31.6	15.8	30.0	1935

Table 18

COMPARISON OF THE DATA

SLOTE VS. FUSSLER AND SIMON[11]
THE IMPACT ON CIRCULATION OF REMOVING VOLUMES
BASED UPON IMPRINT AGE AND SHELF-TIME PERIOD

Criterion	Percentage of Usage Lost					
	Fussler Chicago	Slote				
Imprint Age	Economics	Briarcliff	Tarrytown	Morristown	Trenton	Newark
Oldest:						
25% removed	5.0%	11.2%	9.4%	5.0%	4.4%	3.7%
50% removed	17.0	19.8	21.7	13.7	14.1	12.5
75% removed	28.0	29.4	38.7	30.6	34.9	34.2
Shelf-Time Period						
Longest:						
25% removed	1.0%	1.4%	4.4%	0.5%	1.1%	0.5%
50% removed	8.0	5.9	12.3	6.9	6.7	8.8
75% removed	47.0	28.3	30.8	13.0	20.9	25.2

Table 19

COMPARISON OF THE DATA

SLOTE VS. COWLES COMMISSION LIBRARY*
CUMULATIVE AGE DISTRIBUTION OF BOOKS

	Cowles		Slote, Newark		
Date	At Circulation	In Collection	At Circulation	In Collection	Date
1950–1953	45%	12%	51%	14%	1965–1969
1940–1949	71	38	88	48	1955–1964
1930–1939	90	70	96	73	1945–1954
1920–1929	97	89	99	86	1935–1944
1900–1919	98	96	–	–	1925–1934
Before 1900	100	100	100	100	Before 1925

*Cited in: Gilbert E. Donahue, "The Library of the Cowles Commission for
Research in Economics," Illinois Libraries XXXVII (March 1955), pp. 89-94.

the collection, a wider range of volumes is used and the average book remains on the shelf longer between uses.

Nevertheless, one cannot generalize or predict shelf-time periods based upon the knowledge of the *type* of library being dealt with, for some research and reference collections produce use patterns nearly identical to those produced by some of the fiction collections studied. To cite an example, there were similarities between Silver's mathematics collection and the fiction collection at Trenton (Table 13).

The shelf-time period may relate to the age of the volumes in the collection that circulate. In general, the newer the volumes, the shorter the overall shelf-time periods at circulation. This correlation has some real significance and practical value. For instance, look at these relationships:

	Trueswell		Slote		
At Circulation	Deering	Tech.	Newark	Briarcliff	Morristown
Age of Volume					
2 years or less	16%	29%	39%	68%	60%
Shelf-Time Period					
Retaining 94% of future usage	60 months	24 months	20 months	5 months	1 month

Is it possible that by knowing the imprint age distribution of books circulating one could predict a shelf-time period for weeding? Perhaps one could establish a shelf-time period criterion for libraries by knowing the age distribution of the volumes in the *collection*.

Table 14, dealing with the characteristics of the entire collection, demonstrates the same kind of repeating patterns seen in the other reports. If the same number of current books were purchased each year, and if none were discarded or lost, one would expect that for each five-year period there would be an equal increase in the cumulative percentage of holdings for each period. This was not the case for the libraries reporting. There had been a relatively even growth of imprint age in the collections in the last fifteen or twenty years, but as time passed, the proportion of the holdings of the earlier imprints was reduced appreciably. It is concluded that while recent purchases may have increased, the older books were weeded more heavily than newer works. It can be seen in Table 23 (see page 121) that, although the holdings of older books were relatively small, the usage was relatively even smaller. Thus, in Newark, books over ten years old represented 67 percent of the collection but only 26 percent of the usage. While the age of a volume is not as good a predictor of future use as is the shelf-time period, it still has some value in predicting a need to weed.

Tables 17 and 18 show another close relationship. Table 18 illustrates the impact on circulation of weeding substantial parts of the collection. Once more there were some striking similarities between Fussler's data and that of this researcher.

IN-LIBRARY USE VERSUS CIRCULATION USE

It had been suggested by Fussler and Simon that the in-library use of a volume is similar to the circulation use of the same volume. Even if these uses were identical for circulating volumes, the information would not solve the entire library weeding problem. Certain types of materials do not circulate at all; therefore, no use data is developed for them at circulation. Other types of materials have limited use because they are inaccessible. Rare books, books in locked cases, books used mostly by librarians, etc., would all be difficult to describe in terms of shelf-time period from observations at the circulation desk. Periodicals are an even more difficult problem, since some libraries permit circulation only of older volumes, some permit selective circulation, and some permit no circulation at all.

It is suggested that in-library use be recorded for each volume as it occurs. This can be done by asking patrons not to return materials to the shelves after use. The clerks should record the date of usage before reshelving. In libraries with closed stacks, records of usage can be centralized, making data collection easier to control. Mechanically, the record control can be simplified by using the spine marking system previously discussed.

The practice of browsing calls for more study in order to determine how best to record this kind of in-library use. For example, a book that appears to be useful to a researcher, may be removed from the shelf, studied briefly, and then reshelved. The book has been examined, but should it be considered to have been used?

THE MEANING OF THE WORD "USE"

One of the most provocative problems of libraries is the real meaning of the word "use." While this volume frequently employs the word "use" as a synonym of "circulation," it is apparent that more study is called for in defining what is meant by "library usage" and whether each "use" is to be evaluated as equal to every other "use."

The different types of usage vary greatly. A library may be "used" for educational purposes, or recreational, or informational, etc. Are all types of usage of equal value and worth to society?

Usage is not always visible. A bibliographer who wants to compile a bibliography of "women's liberation" may do so provided she discovers, in a library, that such a work has *not* been done before. In this case, *absence* of a work becomes an important kind of "use" to the bibliographer.

Most use studies disregard the quality of importance of a "use." Is the information to be used for some ultimate benefit to society or for some destructive purpose? Most librarians would accept a value difference between use of a library by George Wallace's would-be assassin and use by a medical researcher trying to cure cancer; When use is measured, do numbers alone reflect the value of such a use? Perhaps one use for a "good" purpose may outweigh all other uses enjoyed by a library.

It becomes clear that even the amount of usage of a given work can vary tremendously either in the library or out. Some books are never looked at again after being checked out of the library. They are carried home and remain untouched until they are returned.

At the other end of the spectrum, some books are read, re-read, outlined, studied, and digested. Many are lent to other readers. Are these two uses equally important for the purposes of determining core collections?

Even if one were to take into consideration the amount of time spent with a volume, problems would arise. Some people read 200 words a minute and others read 2,000 or more! Is the fast reader getting a lower quality of use because his time input is so much less?

This study strongly recommends further study of the quality and meaning of "library use." The "numbers game" presently played by librarians rarely relates to meaningful use.

THE PATTERN OF BOOK USE DESCRIBED

It has long been recognized that there is a pattern of use for books as they are added to a library collection. Almost all the studies have shown heavier use, on the average, in the earlier periods, with a drop in usage as the book gets older. However, there have been many books which always exhibit a high level of use. It is this characteristic of book use patterns that makes age a poor criterion of weeding. If all older books were weeded, a substantial part of the total circulation would still be retained but access to the older editions would be made more difficult. Few librarians would accept this type of weeding.

What really seems to happen in public libraries is that the circulation is made up substantially of the new books (most of which will slowly disappear from circulation use) and a relatively small group of older books that exhibit the same circulation patterns as the new books. From the author's point of view, that is what is meant by a "classic": it is an older book, past its usage age as defined by library usage averages, but circulating as the newer books do. If circulation is accepted as a criterion for defining a "classic," it becomes painfully clear that substantial parts of present classic collections consist of non-classics. In every library observed, at least half the Charles Dickens titles held did not circulate. Generally, *David Copperfield* was the classic and *Dombey and Son* was a candidate for the non-core collection.

There is no such thing as an "average" title. Libraries are dealing with whole collections; yet, from a practical point of view they must deal with each volume according to value. Presume that in a twelve-month period, one book circulates every two months and another not at all. The books together have circulated six times, or an average of three circulations per volume. It is the contention of this work that such an average has no practical value. It highlights the need for a criterion where each volume is judged by its *own usage*, not by some *average* characteristics.

THE EFFECT OF WEEDING ON USAGE

Very little is known about the effect of weeding on use; whether it decreases, increases, or does not change the amount of use. No relevant studies have been found in the literature. Some research in depth is called for in this area. There is some *evidence* that might be considered.

In Harrison, several thousand books, mostly duplicates and older volumes, were removed to a less accessible area, an area of secondary storage. Practically no usage was observed during the year following the move. On the other hand, adult fiction experienced a 6.2 percent proportionate increase when 1,200 volumes were removed. It would be extremely difficult to say that weeding increased the demand. However, it would be equally difficult to disregard the possibility that weeding increased circulation (see Tables 10 and 11).

Another aspect was revealed by the experience of the library in Briarcliff, which increased the McNaughton rental collection since such a high percentage of its total use came from this sub-collection. After it doubled the size of this collection, it experienced a substantial circulation increase in fiction (see page 122). Since the mix of the collection was changed in a way that weeding would have changed it—a higher proportion of heavily used books now existed—it pointed to the possibility that circulation was influenced by a process similar to weeding.

In the study of a older collection in an under-supported library in New Jersey, another visible aspect of the collection became obvious. This collection consisted mostly of books which, had they been in the sample libraries, would have received very little use. Yet, since the acquisitions budget was small, the collection contained older, beat-up volumes past their normal reader interest period. While some of these books were used, the total library patronage was falling off and the use per volume was low. This seemed to indicate that some people will borrow almost anything when they want to read; others will just stop using the library.

Based upon such limited evidence, it was felt that what really happened was that if the normal recreational demand of a library were being met in a relatively satisfactory manner, weeding could increase the circulation immediately. The recreational user often does not look in the card catalog but goes directly to the shelves and selects those books he thinks will satisfy him. The exact titles do not seem to make much difference, since he knows in advance the kinds of books he is likely to find on the shelves. If the collection seems more vital and interesting, and if it contains a *higher proportion* of the kind of books he is interested in, he will borrow more books.

SUMMARY

The public library is in a strange position. As far as the user is concerned, he is getting, at no direct charge, books that he would pay for elsewhere. Yet many choose to pay when their exact needs are not met. Certainly weeding will help increase circulation if the types and quantities of books that replace the weeded volumes attract new segments of the potential clientele of the community. Not only bestsellers, but also specialized collections in art, education, business, etc., might have this effect. Product improvement could be a potent force for increasing library usage, especially when it is combined with a strong effort to acquaint the public with such improvements and changes.

REFERENCES

1. Samuel H. Ranck, "The Problem of the Unused Book," *Library Journal* XXXVI (August 1911), p. 428.

2. Winston Charles Lister, "Least Cost Decision Rules for the Selection of Library Materials for Compact Storage" (unpublished Ph.D. dissertation, Purdue University, 1967), pp. 162-64.

3. Edward A. Silver, "A Quantitative Appraisal of the M.I.T. Science Library Mezzanine with an Application to the Problem of Limited Shelf Space" (unpublished term paper for M.I.T. graduate course 8:75, Operations Research, 1962), p. 38.

4. Ralph Blasingame and others, *The Book Collections in the Public Libraries of the Pottsville Library District: A Date and Subject Distribution Study* (Pottsville, Pa.: Pottsville Free Public Library, 1967), Chart 24.

5. Ibid., Chart 13.

6. Marianne Cooper, "Criteria for Weeding of Collections," *Library Resources and Technical Services* XII (Summer 1968), p. 349.

7. Richard William Trueswell, "User Behavioral Patterns and Requirements and Their Effect on the Possible Applications of Data Processing and Computer Techniques in a University Library" (unpublished Ph.D. dissertation, Northwestern University, 1964), pp. 103-104.

8. Ibid., pp. 96-97.

9. Aridaman K. Jain and others, "A Statistical Study of Book Use Supplemented with a Bibliography of Library Use Studies" (unpublished Ph.D. dissertation, Purdue University, 1967), p. 253, (converted into percentages).

10. A. K. Jain, "Sampling and Short-Period Usage in the Purdue Library," *College and Research Libraries* XXVII (May 1966), p. 217.

11. Herman H. Fussler and Julian L. Simon, *Patterns in the Use of Books in Large Research Libraries* (Chicago: University of Chicago Press, 1969), pp. 49, 51.

CHAPTER 13

HOW TO WEED

SELECTING THE BEST METHOD
FOR DETERMINING SHELF-TIME PERIOD

In order to create the shelf-time period information necessary to weed, one must first study the method of circulation control, to determine whether adequate data currently exists. If it exists, it can be utilized; if it does not exist, the primary use data must be created.

The only method that will collect the data is one that shows dates representing the circulations of a volume. This is usually the case when the book card method of circulation control is being used, although certain computer control systems might also be able to recreate the necessary data. In these cases, Method A or B should be used. Method A, *the book card method*, takes longer, is safer, and involves the most computation. Method B, *the simplified method*, can give the same results with much less work, if the method is carefully followed.

If the necessary circulation information is not available, it must be created, a process that may take anywhere from six months to five or more years to complete. Method C, *the spine marking method*, creates the data in a visible and obvious fashion; it may be used for non-circulating material as well as circulating. It simplifies weeding, and it visibly indicates how heavily or lightly the various parts of the collection are being used.

Method D, *the substitute book card method*, is recommended only for libraries that object to spine marking. In effect, it records each circulation and temporarily attaches the information to the volume circulating. When weeding is completed, the records are removed and the system discontinued.

For the long run, the method used to control circulation should indicate the volume's circulating dates in the volume itself.

The Book Card Method. The book card method of use reconstruction was the method used in the *Five Library Study*. The book card method records each circulation on the book card. Usually, the card is stored in the book and removed at the circulation station after the borrower's identification number (sometimes his name and address) and the due-dates have been stamped. Due-dates may be stamped manually or by machine. These book cards are then held at the circulation desk, filed by due-date, and reslipped into book pockets as the volumes are returned by the borrowers. The book card usually reflects the circulation history of a book.

The method of identifying core collections is to observe the book cards from volumes being charged out at the circulation desk. As books are circulated, a consecutive group of four to five hundred cards should be observed and the pertinent information recorded. The books should not be reslipped until the data is tabulated. A table should be created to show to which shelf-time cell each volume is to be assigned (see Appendix B, page 149). To make this assignment, the proper date must be selected from the book card.

1. Selecting the significant due-date. Following is an example of information that may exist on a specific book card of a book that circulates for 28 days:

> January 3, 1973
> March 5, 1973
> August 11, 1973
> December 29, 1973

The shelf-time period on December 1, 1973, is determined as follows: the latest due-date on the card, December 29, 1973, has just been added to the card as the book circulated; it is not used in the computation, since it represents the end of a book's stay on the shelf, which is already known to be December 1, 1973, the day this entry was made. The second significant date is the charge-out that occurred prior to this current usage. August 11, 1973, represents the significant due-date, the previous time this volume circulated. It is this date that determines the cell assignment.

2. Tabulating the data. Create a summary chart of cell assignments as follows: (as explained in Appendix B, page 146ff.). Assign each volume to its proper cell, using the significant due-date.

Due-Date Describing this Shelf-Time Period	Shelf-Time Period (Months)	Volumes Assigned to this Cell	Total
11/9/73–12/28/73	0	̶1̶1̶1̶1̶ ̶1̶1̶1̶1̶ ̶1̶1̶1̶1̶ 11	17
10/10/73–11/8/73	1	̶1̶1̶1̶1̶ 111	8
9/10/73–10/9/73	2	̶1̶1̶1̶1̶	5
8/11/73–9/11/73	3	111	3
7/12/73–8/10/73	4		
6/12/73–7/11/73	5	1	1
5/13/73–6/11/73	6		
4/13/73–5/12/73	7	1	1
3/14/73–4/12/73	8		
2/13/73–3/13/73	9		
1/14/73–2/12/73	10	1	1

The counted samples should be summarized and percentages computed. A 377-volume sampling might have a list of shelf-time periods similar to the following:

Shelf-Time Period	No. of Volumes in this Period	Volumes in this Period or Shorter	
		No.	Percent
0	328	328	86.7
1	23	351	92.9
2	14	365	96.8
3	3	368	97.6
4	3	371	98.4
5	3	374	99.2
6			
7			
8			
9	1	375	99.5
10			
11	2	377	100.0

One can now select the cut-point, as described by shelf-time period. Thus, if one wishes to retain 98.4 percent of the circulation, one would retain all the volumes in the *collection* having a shelf-time period of four months or less. All volumes having a due-date of 7/11/73 or earlier are in the non-core. This computation predicts the future use of the volumes in the present collection, based upon past use patterns as reflected by the variable shelf-time period.

The Simplified Method. Because the book card method seemed complex and time-consuming, some effort was made to simplify it. It was discovered that neither the loan period nor the adjustment of due-dates for any reason has any significant effect on practical weeding decisions. In addition, creating monthly cells turned out to be unnecessary, as did most of the tabulation. The simplified method is used as follows:

1. Collect the book cards from 400 consecutively circulating volumes. Keep these cards intact by not reslipping them into book card pockets until the final data is computed. If exactly 400 cards are collected, the procedure is simplified.

2. Determine the exact level of use to be retained—say, 99 percent.

3. Multiply the sample number (400) by the percentage *not* being retained. In this example, 400 is multiplied by 1 percent giving the number 4.

4. Remove all book cards of books having shorter loan periods if more than one loan period is utilized. All these were found to belong to the core.

5. Shuffle through the cards, observing the significant dates (the ones just prior to the current due-date). Arbitrarily select an older date that seems to be 7th or 8th from the oldest and then list chronologically all the older significant dates (as below). If the arbitrarily selected date does not cause a listing of enough older dates (4 for a 99 percent keeping; 20 for a 95 percent keeping), then start the list with a date around 30 days more recent, and keep advancing that date until enough dates have been listed. For example, the dates written may look as follows:

> August 1, 1961
> September 20, 1964
> January 12, 1966
> October 7, 1970
> July 13, 1971
> July 30, 1971
> August 12, 1971
> September 8, 1971
> (the 392 other dates are *not* tabulated).

The 99 percent keeping cut-point would be October 7, 1970. By reshuffling through the book cards, make sure again that all pertinent dates *before* October 7, 1970, have been listed.

6. Use the date found as the cut-point, weeding out of the *collection* all volumes whose most recent previous circulation date is the same as or older than this cut-point date.

The Spine Marking Method. This is the best method to use when the book cards are not date-stamped and there is no way to recreate use information from them. It is also of value for use on non-circulating materials. This method requires that the spine of circulating books be marked with a very visible stick-on label. As new volumes are added to the collection, each should be similarly marked to prevent its being weeded before it has had a chance to circulate. All markings should be applied in exactly the same location on each volume. To be sure that none remain unmarked, it is a good practice to double-check volumes as they are returned to the library (i.e., during the discharge process, before reshelving).

When it is clear that very few books are being circulated without spine marks, the circulating station should take a count of 400 or 500 consecutive charge outs, tabulating the percentage of spine-marked volumes. The library must determine in advance the keeping level. If the predetermined keeping level is 95 percent, then when 95 percent of the volumes of one class come to circulation with the spine marking, all volumes on the shelf without the spine marking can be weeded.

This method is the simplest way to weed. Weeding decisions can be made without removing volumes from the shelf. The principal disadvantage, however, is that it takes time—perhaps several years—to reach the desired percentage.

An advantage of the method is that it can be used continuously. After the library has been completely weeded, and only volumes with spine marks exist, the spines can be marked in another color as the books circulate; then, when 95 percent of the volumes come to the circulation desk with this mark, weeding may be undertaken once more.

The Substitute Book Card Method. Apply the circulation dates to volumes in some way, solely for the purpose of weeding. This involves dating all of the volumes in the collection at the start of the program and then dating each volume as it is added to the collection. This may be done by temporarily attaching to each volume a slip of paper on which the date of each circulation or use is noted. At the circulation station, these slips are periodically observed and records are kept on the percentages of the circulating volumes that have been used since starting the study.

This method, in theory, is very similar to the book card method; it merely recreates information normally found on book cards. At any future time, a shelf-time cut-period can be established by listing all the dates on the paper slips as in the book card method. The charging systems that dot the back of book cards used in transaction card circulation systems can be used for this substitute method.

HOW TO PREDICT THE NUMBER OF BOOKS
WHICH WILL BE WEEDED AT A GIVEN LEVEL
OF FUTURE USE

The four methods above are adequate for weeding, but they do not indicate *how much* weeding will take place. This can be determined only by first describing the *collection* in terms of the same variable, as was done above for volumes circulating.

1. In the book card method, a systematic sample of 400 should be taken of the entire collection, identifying the shelf-time period distribution of the volumes. Remember that "the entire collection" also includes the volumes in circulation. The same kind of tabulation made for circulating volumes is created and the percentages compared. If 98 percent of the books at circulation have a six-month shelf-time period, while only 50 percent of the volumes in the collection have the same characteristic, then the library will retain 98 percent of the use with 50 percent of the volumes.

2. In the simplified method, again a systematic sample of approximately 400 is taken from the collection. Total tabulation is unnecessary, and shorter loan period volumes need not be tabulated either. All volumes having a due-date older than the cut-point date should be *counted*. This number divided by 400 will give the percentage to be weeded when using the previously selected cut-date.

3. In the spine marking method, in a small collection, it is easiest just to count the marked and non-marked books in the collection and create percentage

ratios. This can also be done by sampling, using about 400 volumes selected by a systematic sampling with a random start to such sampling.

4. In the substitute book card method, cut-dates are counted, as in the simplified method, by sampling the collection as in the book card method above.

DIFFERENT CLASSES OF BOOKS

As mentioned earlier, different classes of books are likely to have different cut-points at the same level of usage. In each of the above methods, these classifications can be divided as finely as one wishes. For example, European travel books could be handled as one class, Asian travel as another. It simply means that in creating the data, the classes must be differentiated at circulation, when tabulating shelf-time characteristics.

SUGGESTIONS FOR WEEDING IN GENERAL—
A NEW WEEDING DEPARTMENT

A number of aspects of weeding become apparent when research is undertaken. For example, libraries frequently have librarians doing the daily acquisitions work, but weeding is rarely done on a daily basis. In the maintenance of a library collection, weeding is as important as acquisition. Though libraries of all sizes should provide for weeding services, full-time weeding librarians and weeding departments are indicated for large libraries, where weeding should be a continuous activity.

Before a weeding department is established, the objectives and the standards of performance of such a department should be determined. The weeding department should be charged with the establishment of weeding criteria, the determination of keeping levels, and the physical process of book removal. In addition to making provisions for the final disposition of books, the weeding department should determine the mechanics of performing the work.

The authority of the weeding department should extend to all related departments—such as the circulation desk, where data is collected, and book preparation, where arrangements and designs for creating necessary data must start.

The relationship between the weeding department and other related departments is summarized as follows:

Circulation. Must keep records, tabulate results of dates or spine marking. A double-check should be made by clerks reshelving books—whether books from circulation or volumes removed from the stacks but not circulating.

Book preparation or repair. Must date or spine-mark all new additions, so that the first appearance on the shelves can be indicated. As cards are replaced, information must be carried forward.

Acquisitions. Information, especially in the spine-marking system, is available on the needs of the library. Weeding should keep acquisitions advised as to classes of books in small supply and heavy demand.

Administration. Needs adequate budget and personnel for weeding operations. Must provide secondary storage for volumes when discarding is not called for.

Cataloging. Catalogs must be changed to reflect weeding activity, either by pulling cards or by noting new locations of volumes.

CONTINUOUS WEEDING

Continuous weeding should be the aim of every library, whether weeded volumes are discarded or stored in secondary locations. Libraries using the book card method should divide the collection, by classes, into twelve sections, each containing approximately the same number of books; one such section should be weeded each month. Since data for the cut-point can be created most precisely only with a substantial sample (say 400 volumes), one section can be weeded, while the next class is being sampled.

When using spine marking, continuous weeding must take another form. One relatively long time period must pass while the data is first being developed. Once an indication of shelf-time has been received, the work should be done promptly. Again, the collection can be divided by class. Since the entire weeding operation is simplified in this method, it is suggested that the weeding department be responsible for marking the spines, partially relieving the regular circulation staff of this function. The weeding department should also do the necessary record keeping that signals when the cut-point for the desired level of future use has been identified.

CHAPTER 14

WEEDING LIBRARY COLLECTIONS—SUMMARIZED

This volume has contained a number of opinions and findings that resulted from either the research projects, the study of the literature of weeding, or practical experience in weeding libraries. Included are research findings, basic concepts, and practical advice, as well as new ideas on the subject. This chapter summarizes the major suggestions and recommendations contained throughout the volume.

CONCEPTS AND ASSUMPTIONS

1. Weeding is called for to maximize the use of the library's physical resources, to improve ease of usage, and to bring about lower costs and higher levels of service.

2. Present holdings tend to be historic accidents, dependent upon what has been stolen as well as what has been purchased, built by a series of different acquisition librarians with changing objectives and budgets.

3. "Weeding" means removal from the primary stack area: to some secondary area, to some central repository, or as discards.

4. Secondary access will not prevent successful research work.

5. Regional responsibility should be set up for the preservation and distribution of works that are used relatively rarely, weeded by others.

6. Subjective weeding criteria tend to be invalid, contradictory, and a poor approach to the problem of weeding.

7. Much more sophisticated costing is needed to determine the real cost of weeding and storage.

USAGE AND SHELF-TIME PERIOD

1. Those books that have the least likelihood of being used should be weeded from the primary collection.

2. Substantial weeding, if shelf-time period is used as a criterion, does not reduce circulation.

3. Such weeding *may*, in fact, promote circulation.

4. Such weeding may be done either by class or for the library as a whole, and neither will have a harmful effect on circulation.

5. Library subject or class holdings are not in proportion to library usage.

6. New standards for weeding ought to be created, with the goal of retaining a core collection (the useful part of the collection) that is likely to meet 95 to 99 percent of future demands made upon the collection.

USAGE AND IMPRINT AGE

1. The imprint age of a volume is a valid but impractical weeding criterion as compared to shelf-time period.

2. Using imprint age as a sole criterion for weeding will weed many classics from primary collections.

SHELF-TIME PERIOD

1. Shelf-time period is valid, accurate, and by far the best criterion for weeding.

2. Reference collections tend to have longer shelf-time periods than non-reference collections.

EVALUATION

1. Collections can be evaluated on the basis of how closely the collection matches the circulation; the closer they are the better the collection.

2. Spine marking is an excellent tool for uncovering areas for acquisition, since the concentration of spine-marked volumes on the shelves indicates greater usage and a need for more volumes of that class of books.

METHODOLOGY

1. Shelf-time period data can be created quickly and simply; libraries with the book card system of circulation control use the "simplified method" of developing the cut-off date for weeding.

2. Non-circulating books should be weeded and use data should be recorded by library staff before books used within the library are reshelved.

3. Monthly or seasonal use patterns exist in libraries and must be taken into consideration when establishing shelf-time cut-off periods for weeding.

4. Circulation systems must establish use and acquisition date information so that shelf-time period can be computed easily.

    a) This includes dating all new books when they are first put on the shelves.

    b) It means the last date must be carried forward to book cards when such cards are replaced.

5. For libraries that cannot recreate records of past use, the spine marking method is simple, economical, and useful for weeding.

    a) The spine marking system is a simplified method of weeding.

    b) There are serious mechanical problems involved in getting spines marked with consistency and accuracy.

    c) Different classes of books have different use patterns.

    d) A machine ought to be developed that automatically marks spines when charging out books.

THE FUTURE

1. Weeding is as important as acquiring and should be done on a regular, continuous basis by personnel assigned solely to this function.

2. A weeding department should be created in large libraries.

INTRODUCTION TO APPENDICES

These appendices are designed for the librarian who wishes to know more of the technical details of the weeding studies. They are meant to give some in-depth information on matters covered in certain previous chapters. Up to this point, this volume can be used as a practical guide to weeding library collections. For a more thorough, complete, and detailed understanding of certain aspects of weeding, these appendices should be helpful.

APPENDIX A

THE QUANTITATIVE FINDINGS OF THE STUDIES—
THEIR USES, MEANING, AND VALUE

SHELF-TIME PERIOD

One of the basic findings highlighted the fact that the shelf-time characteristics of a sample library could really define two overlapping but different collections: the collection that tends to circulate (called the core collection) and the collection that tends not to circulate (called the non-core collection). Table 1 (page 30), helps to identify these collections and shows their interrelationship. Thus, using Briarcliff as an example, at the 96 percent level of future use (the circulation sample), 56 percent of the collection is in the core and the remainder (44 percent) in the non-core collection. For any level of desired usage, the likely core and non-core collections can be estimated.

Once it has been created, this table can be used in a variety of ways. If a specific amount of *shelf space* must be made available through weeding, it could predict with some reliability and precision what percentage of the volumes in the collection will be removed from primary storage areas at the various usage levels. If a known level of *future* usage is desired, it can indicate the likely *size* of the core collection at that level.

It can also indicate the *quality* of the collection in one important respect. The closer the collection matches the circulation, the more efficient is the collection. In an idealized circulating collection, all the volumes would be circulated.

Another value of such a table could be a greater understanding of the *character* of collections compared to other libraries. Table 20 has been recast, disregarding the shelf-time periods but listing the collection characteristics as compared to circulation by the percentages of use satisfied. At the point that they satisfy 97 percent of the circulation demand, it was found the percentage of the present collection needed ranges from 56 percent to 82 percent.

Another suggestion for using the figures developed in the *Five Library Study* relates to the impact of the "number of circulations per volume" on the *length of the shelf-time periods*. Some serious study is called for in this area. Table 21 shows the data. There seemed to be a relationship between the number of uses for each volume and the shelf-time cut-points. The more uses per volume, in general, the shorter the shelf-time period. In Harrison, with 4.5 circulations

Table 20

**PERCENTAGE OF THE COLLECTION NEEDED TO SATISFY
CIRCULATION DEMAND, FIVE LIBRARIES**

% of Circulation Satisfied	% of the Present Collection Needed to Satisfy this Circulation Demand				
	Briarcliff	Tarrytown	Morristown	Trenton	Newark
50					14
60				14	19
70	20	25		20	22
80	31	38		27	31
85	37	47	37	31	40
90	47	57	46	45	47
95	54	72	54	63	60
97	64	82	56	67	70
99	84	96	72	80	74

Table 21

**AVERAGE NUMBER OF CIRCULATIONS PER YEAR
VERSUS SHELF-TIME PERIOD, FIVE LIBRARIES**

	Morristown	Briarcliff	Tarrytown	Newark	Trenton
Average No. of Circulations per Volume per Year	6.2	3.5	2.8	1.5	1.4
Shelf-Time Period (in mos.) Likely to Retain 95% of the Circulation	2	6	1	23	23

per fiction volume, it was estimated that the shelf-time period for the 95 percent level of future usage would fall between 4 and 5 months. In fact, it was 6 months. While such data cannot predict the period exactly, it is possible that it could have some practical benefit.

In addition, the circulation per volume might be used to evaluate a collection. It is likely that there exists a "most efficient level of book holdings." With too few volumes, a very high use-per-volume will occur. Conversely, when a collection has large numbers of volumes that are never used, it likely has too many books for maximum efficiency, and the use-per-volume will be low.

If a librarian knows 1) the percentage of the total collection that is in circulation at any one time, and 2) the ratio of the holdings in a class related to the percentage of total use represented by that class, he is probably on his way to evaluating how many books should be in an efficient library.

If "too much" of a core collection is in circulation at any one time, there is an apparent weakness in the collection. It indicates that some readers must be finding the library unsatisfactory. It is possible that, through research, an idealized circulation percentage could be established.

An example of the range of possibilities can be found in the Harrison Public Library, where about 35 percent of the adult fiction volumes are generally out in circulation, while only 12 percent of the adult biographies are out. It is likely that the library needs more fiction and less biography in order to be more efficient.

Little is known about the relationship between holdings and use. Table 22 shows this relationship in three libraries. In each case fiction is under-represented in the collection—i.e., there is a higher percentage of use than one would expect, if use paralleled holdings. However, the table shows each library with rather similar usage—from 30 percent to 35.4 percent, with relatively small impact indicated by the quantity of the holdings.

Observing the concentration of spine markings of volumes on the shelves in a spine-marking system allows one to predict rather accurately which classes of books have the highest percentages out in circulation. With few dotted books on the shelves, there are few in circulation. Thus, certain circulation characteristics are usually revealed by shelf-time characteristics, and such information can be used in acquiring new volumes.

As has been pointed out previously (Table 12), there is a considerable imbalance between the holdings of the Harrison Public Library and the usage pattern. It was pointed out that 25.8 percent of the adult holdings are fiction but 48.2 percent of the circulation comes from that class. (After weeding the fiction, this imbalance became even greater, since fiction circulation increased after 1,200 volumes had been removed.)

Table 22

PERCENTAGE OF USE VERSUS PERCENTAGE OF HOLDINGS
MORRISTOWN–TARRYTOWN–BRIARCLIFF

	% of Total Holdings Represented by Fiction	% of Total Use Represented by Fiction
Morristown	9.1	30.0
Tarrytown	28.2	35.4
Briarcliff	24.4	35.1

IMPRINT AGE

The basic data accumulated on the use of imprint age as the variable, studied both at circulation and for the collection as a whole, is shown in Table 23. Even where the collection is heavily supplied with older books, the drop-off is severe.

For instance, in Trenton, 13 percent of the collection consists of imprints from 1965 to 1969 and 17 percent from 1960 to 1964, yet 52 percent of the usage was from the first and smaller group, and only 21 percent of the usage from the older but considerably larger group. Again, as the book imprints get older, the usage drops even more severely. Although 1955 to 1959 is represented in the collection by 16 percent of the works, again the usage went down to 11 percent. There is no question that we can see a use imbalance in which a definable part of the collection is under-represented in usage.

Another interesting but misleading observation is that apparently some of the very old books are never used. In an experiment in which much larger numbers of samples were observed, the earliest imprint date uncovered was considerably older than the date shown in these limited samples. The imprint age of the oldest book, both in the collection and at circulation, would almost surely be extended if the *entire* circulation and the *entire* collection were examined.

The most obvious conclusion that can be drawn from these tables is that age is not as useful a predictor of future use as is shelf-time period. Briarcliff could weed, at the 99 percent keeping level, 16 percent of the volumes when the variable shelf-time period is used, against only 4 percent when age is used. Thus, one method would result in four times as much weeding as the other.

Another observation is that, in each of these public libraries, over 50 percent of the fiction usage was accounted for by books with an imprint date under five years old; 73 percent or more came from books with an imprint date ten years old or less; over 84 percent came from volumes with a 15-year-old or less imprint date. It is thus apparent that the newer books represent most of the usage.

Table 23

THE IMPRINT AGE OF THE CIRCULATION AND THE COLLECTION
SAMPLES COMPARED (%), FIVE LIBRARIES

Year of Imprint	Briarcliff		Tarrytown		Morristown		Trenton		Newark	
	Circulation	Collection	Circulation	Collection	Circulation	Collection	Circulation	Collection	Circulation	Collection
1965–1969*	73	30	58	21	69	28	52	13	51	14
1960–1964	84	59	75	44	84	49	73	30	74	33
1955–1959	91	78	86	62	90	60	84	46	88	48
1950–1954	94	86	91	75	92	67	90	59	94	64
1945–1949	96	91	94	82	93	72	94	71	96	73
1940–1944	98	93	96	88	96	76	96	76	98	81
1935–1939	99	96	97	90	–	81	97	80	99	86
1930–1934	–	98	98	93	98	85	99	86	–	89
1925–1929	–	–	–	96	–	87	–	89	–	93
1920–1924	–	99	–	97	99	90	–	92	–	94
1915–1919	–	–	100	98	–	92	–	94	–	95
1910–1914	–	–	–	–	–	93	–	96	–	–
1905–1909	100	–	–	–	–	94	–	97	–	–
1900–1904	–	–	–	–	100	96	100	98	100	96
Before 1900	–	100	–	100	–	100	–	100	–	100

*Part of year 1969 only.

In every case, the books in the newest group (1965 to 1969 imprint date) had greater usage than would be expected if usage were in proportion to holdings. Except for Trenton and Newark, in the second cell (1960 to 1964) the percentage of holdings increase is greater than use increase. Beyond that date, with rare exception, the circulation is always disproportionate to the holdings—a clear indication that too many older imprints were being retained. A typical example might be found in Briarcliff, when comparing 1950 to 1954 with 1955 to 1959. In this step, there is a 3 percent increase in the circulation, but an 8 percent increase in the collection. It is possible that circulation could be increased by increasing the proportion of newer imprints in the collection.

There is some evidence that increasing these proportions might be effective. In Briarcliff, the McNaughton rental collection was increased in May 1969 from 250 volumes to 500 volumes. The volumes had all been published within the previous few months. All other normal purchase patterns were continued as before. In subsequent years, an increase in fiction circulation was noted and such circulation was retained. The figures reported are as follows:

Year	Total Circulation	Fiction Circulation
1968	35,293	12,399
1969	33,125	11,787*
1970	33,459	13,112
1971	35,891	13,540
1972	36,859	14,429

*New volumes added in May.

This fiction use increase reversed a persistent trend of reduced fiction use. Apparently, the increase was made partially at the expense of non-fiction circulation. By 1970, not only was the fiction usage still increasing, but the total usage in the library was increasing.

To return to the imprint date information once more, another interesting pattern can be observed. For the five libraries, the purchases made during the last two five-year periods were similar. In Briarcliff, for example, 30 percent of its collection was bought in the last five years and 29 percent in the previous five years. It was assumed that no significant weeding of these materials took place and that newly acquired books had very recent imprint dates.

With the exception of Trenton and Newark, the holdings for the next few time periods, representing earlier imprints, dropped off radically. Trenton and Newark both visualized themselves as libraries of permanent record, never discarding the last copy of any title. The others, which were most recreationally oriented, had apparently weeded old imprints much more heavily.

Even Trenton and Newark, however, experienced a continuous and substantial drop-off in holdings as imprints got older. Perhaps lower budgets before, during, and right after the war meant that fewer books were purchased at the earlier dates. It is likely that all these libraries had done some weeding, and that they tended to weed the older books. Perhaps because fewer books were published in earlier years, fewer were purchased.

Whatever the causes, almost all the libraries observed reflected the same kind of uneven age distribution for fiction. Blasingame also found this kind of uneven distribution in his sample libraries (see Table 14, page 96).

The striking similarity between Blasingame's data and this author's data must not obscure the fact that Blasingame also found different patterns and that some of his samples ran counter to the above trend. Conflicting data points out the danger and fallacy in trying to generalize from one sample of five libraries.

Classics present a special condition. Newer editions of classics showed the greatest use. In a public library, the newer volumes of Shakespeare, with recent imprint dates, circulate heavily, while the older volumes tend to remain on the shelves unused. However, in the five libraries, almost no one was willing to weed the *unused* older editions of those works. This is one of the exceptions to a conventional weeder's focus on imprint age.

IMPRINT DATA VS. SHELF-TIME PERIOD

A major finding of this study is that shelf-time period is a "better" weeding criterion than the imprint age of the volumes. As can be seen in Table 24, at both the 95 percent and 99 percent level of future circulation, using the criterion of shelf-time period requires fewer books to satisfy reader demand than using imprint date. In Morristown, at the 99 percent level, only 9.9 percent of the books could be removed by applying the imprint age of the volume as the weeding criterion, whereas 34.7 percent could be weeded when using the shelf-time period criterion. In a fiction collection of 8,748 volumes, 3,035 could be weeded using the better criterion while only 866 could be removed using the other criterion, with *the future circulation remaining at the same level*. Thus, in this example, 3½ times as many volumes could be weeded without any unfavorable impact upon the collection.

Further, it can be seen in Table 24 that from a practical point of view, at the 99 percent level of retained usage, weeding would hardly be justified in three of the libraries, if imprint age were to be used as the weeding criterion. Briarcliff, Tarrytown, and Trenton would remove so few books as to make the effort uneconomical. With only 4 percent of the collection to be weeded, the cost of such an effort (which requires looking at the other 96 percent of the collection as well) would be excessive. Added to this must be the cost of creating the cut-off date.

Tarrytown is the only library in which it might be inefficient to weed using the shelf-time period criterion at the 99 percent keeping level. The core collection was indicated at 93.7 percent, almost the same size as if imprint of the volumes were used as the weeding criterion. An explanation of this is that just prior to this study Tarrytown had weeded many of its older imprints from the collection. However, because subjective criteria had been used, the library had been weeded *inefficiently*. Another 29.1 percent of the volumes might have been weeded, still retaining 95 percent of the present usage.

Table 24

AGE OF IMPRINT VERSUS SHELF-TIME PERIOD FOR
IDENTIFYING CORE COLLECTIONS, FIVE LIBRARIES

	Percent of Present Collection in Core Collection	
	---	---
	Selected By	
At Approximately the 95% Level of Future Use	Shelf-Time Period	Imprint Date
Morristown	56.2	75.0
Briarcliff	56.4	87.3
Tarrytown	70.9	85.5
Newark	61.3	70.9
Trenton	55.2	72.9
At Approximately the 99% Level of Future Use		
Morristown	65.3	90.1
Briarcliff	78.6	96.0
Tarrytown	93.7	95.7
Newark	73.6	89.4
Trenton	75.2	96.4

It is of interest to observe the characteristics of the retained core collections under the two methods of weeding. In Morristown, at the 96.8 percent level of future use, the shelf-time period identified 56.2 percent of the collection to be retained as a core, while the imprint age identified 75 percent at approximately the same level of usage (95 percent). This meant that using imprint age as the criterion retained an additional 18.8 percent of the collection in the core. This 18.8 percent difference was increased to 24.6 percent after books that did not have enough data available to produce both criteria were omitted from the useful sample (see Table 25). While this distorts the results somewhat, it does not change the pattern that emerges indicating different core collections.

Table 25 shows 1941 as the imprint date cut-point. All books with a 1941 or more recent imprint date would have to be retained in the core. All volumes with an older imprint date would have to be weeded. It can be seen from this tabulation that using these different criteria resulted in substantial differences in the specific volumes to be weeded. Obviously, the imprint criterion retains the same volumes as the shelf-time period criterion for all books with imprint date newer than 1940. Up to that date, all books in the first core are also in the second.

Table 25

COMPARISON OF CORE COLLECTIONS AS IDENTIFIED BY
SHELF-TIME PERIOD AND BY MOST RECENT
IMPRINT DATE, MORRISTOWN

Year of Imprint	Percentage of Volumes to be Kept in the Core Collection Selected by Shelf-Time Period	Percentage of Volumes to be Kept in the Core Collection Selected by Imprint Date
1969	100.0	100.0
1968	100.0	100.0
1967	92.3	100.0
1966	69.4	100.0
1965	64.3	100.0
1964	66.7	100.0
1963	47.8	100.0
1962	68.4	100.0
1961	45.0	100.0
1960	38.9	100.0
1959	33.3	100.0
1958	66.7	100.0
1957	54.5	100.0
1956	33.3	100.0
1955	57.1	100.0
1954	33.3	100.0
1953	55.5	100.0
1952	50.0	100.0
1951	37.5	100.0
1950	40.0	100.0
1949	37.5	100.0
1948	0.0	100.0
1947	33.3	100.0
1946	50.0	100.0
1945	100.0	100.0
1944	40.0	100.0
1943	0.0	100.0
1942	0.0	100.0
1941	33.3	100.0
1936–1940	50.0	0.0
1931–1935	28.6	0.0
1926–1930	26.3	0.0
1921–1925	30.0	0.0
1916–1920	23.1	0.0
1911–1915	22.2	0.0
1906–1910	25.0	0.0
1901–1905	66.7	0.0
1896–1900	11.1	0.0
1891–1895	0.0	0.0
1866–1890	12.5	0.0
1865 and before	40.0	0.0
Total	51.1	75.7

The opposite is true, however, for older imprints. None of the volumes retained in the shelf-time period core are in the imprint core when the imprint is before 1941. Here is where the great difference is observable. Using the imprint age criterion weeds a number of volumes that would actually have substantial circulation.

It can be observed from Table 25 that there were only four cases in which the same volumes in the core collections were selected by both of these criteria. For 1968, 1969, and 1945, both methods retain 100 percent of the volumes in the core. This information has a practical use; when using the shelf-time period criterion to weed, one can retain automatically all newer volumes without checking their date of last use. The only other case of similarity is related to the dates 1891 to 1895, where neither core kept any of those volumes. In actually weeding this collection, it is very likely that at least a few books of this description would have been retained under the shelf-time period criterion.

The substantial differences in the two core collections have been summarized in Table 26. Table 26 summarizes Table 25 by totalling the number of volumes in each quartile or fourth of the sample, as described by the imprint age of the volumes. A number of valuable characteristics can be identified in this table.

First of all, under the preferred method of selection (shelf-time), 228 volumes would provide the same amount of future usage as would 336 volumes retained by the rejected criterion for selection (imprint). This means an increase of 50 percent in the number of relatively useless volumes being retained.

Second, age was a strong predictor of future usage *on an average*. It can be seen that when shelf-time period is used as the predictor, in the first quartile (the youngest imprints) twice as many volumes were being retained as in the much older third quartile. In each older imprint age cell, the number of volumes to be retained gets smaller. But some of these old imprints circulated just as if they had newer imprint dates. In the last quartile, some 26 useful books that are likely to be used would have been weeded under the imprint age criterion.

Third, the range of years gets longer in each quartile cell as the imprint age gets older. The first cell combines four years, the next five years, the next twenty years, and the last perhaps one hundred years. This is a reconfirmation of the finding that *on an average* older books circulate less than newer books. However, Table 25 shows that such usage does not decrease evenly, year by year. For example, 33.3 percent of the books with a 1959 imprint were used, while 50 percent of the 1946 books and 100 percent of the 1945 books were used. One might say that there was a strong *tendency* for usage to reduce with age but there was no *certainty* that this would happen.

CUT-OFF POINTS

Shelf-Time Period. From a practical point of view, a librarian should find valuable a specific criterion that would indicate exactly what to weed. This is called the "cut-off point." Specific, detailed, objective criteria replace the vague and subjective values now used in most weeding.

Table 26

COMPARISON OF CORE COLLECTIONS AS IDENTIFIED BY SHELF-TIME PERIOD AND BY MOST RECENT IMPRINT DATE: BY IMPRINT DATE QUARTILES, MORRISTOWN

Quartile*	Imprint Year Included in This Quartile	Number of Volumes in Core Collection Identified by Shelf-Time Period	% of Volumes in Core Identified by Shelf-Time Period	% of Volumes in Core Identified by Imprint Age
1st	1966-1969	93 of 111	83.8	100.0
2nd	1961-1965	59 of 111	52.2	100.0
3rd	1942-1960	47 of 111	42.3	100.0
4th	1865-1941	29 of 111	26.1	2.7

*Total sample 444 volumes, divided into four groups by imprint date.

Table 27 gives two of these cut-off points in detail. When dealing with the shelf-time period criterion, the cut-off point is given in months; that is, the number of months a book remains on the shelf unused. Volumes that have a shorter shelf-time period are then identified as being in the core collection and those with longer shelf-time periods, in the non-core or weedable collection.

For example, in Tarrytown, in order to retain 95 percent of the desired future use, the cut-off point is 12 months. To retain 99 percent of the future use, the cut-off point is 42 months. Three further observations might be made about the data observed in this part of the study.

1. It can be seen that the pre-selected percentages were not all exactly 95 percent, but were frequently fractional percentages. This characteristic is likely to occur depending upon the techniques used to compute the cut-point. In this study, the cut-points were observed in certain arbitrary cells, described elsewhere, so that the cut-points could be stated in months.

2. There seemed to be a meaningful relationship between the cut-point found at the 95 percent level of future use and that found at the 99 percent level (see page 129).

Table 27

CUT-POINTS AND CORE COLLECTION SIZE–AT 95% AND 99% RETENTION, FIVE LIBRARIES

Identifying the Core Collection by Shelf-Time Period	Morristown	Briarcliff	Tarrytown	Newark	Trenton
1. Pre-selected percent of the circulation to be retained to 95% nearest cell.	96.8	95.5	95.0	95.1	95.1
2. Cut-off shelf-time period in months likely to retain this desired percent of future circulation.	2 mo.	6 mo.	12 mo.	23 mo.	23 mo.
3. Percent of present collection to be retained in the core collection.	56.2	56.4	70.9	61.3	55.2
4. Pre-selected percent of the circulation to be retained nearest cell to 99%.	99.2	98.9	99.0	99.0	98.9
5. Cut-off as in No. 2 above.	5 mo.	14 mo.	42 mo.	40 mo.	70 mo.
6. Percent of present collection to be retained.	65.3	78.6	93.7	73.6	75.2

Identifying the Core Collection by Imprint Dates	Morristown	Briarcliff	Tarrytown	Newark	Trenton
1. Pre-selected percent of the circulation to be retained—95%.	95.0	95.4	95.0	95.0	95.3
2. Cut-off imprint date to retain this percent of the circulation.	1941	1949	1942	1947	1943
3. Percent of present collection to be retained.	75.0	87.3	85.5	70.9	72.9
4. Pre-selected percent of the circulation to be retained—99%.	99.1	98.5	99.5	98.9	99.1
5. Cut-off imprint date to retain this percent of the circulation.	1920	1935	1925	1930	1905
6. Percent of present collection to be retained.	90.1	96.0	95.7	89.4	96.7

Library	Cut-Point, Described in Months	
	95% Level	99% Level
Morristown	2	5
Briarcliff	6	14
Tarrytown	12	42
Newark	23	40
Trenton	23	70

Without reducing this to a precise average, it can be seen that the shelf-time period for 99 percent keeping level is approximately 2½ times greater than the cut-off point for the 95 percent keeping level. It is likely that when creating such cut-points where no helpful information exists, no great danger would be encountered in tripling the time duration of the cut-point of the 95 percent level with some confidence that at least 99 percent of the future use would be preserved. This would save several years of record keeping or other mechanical processing. If this triple rule had been used on the five libraries, the resultant core would have kept the following amount of future circulation:

Percent of Use Retained by Tripling the Shelf-Time Period
Developed for the 95% Level of Use

	Retention
	Circulation Retained to Nearest Percent
Morristown	99
Briarcliff	99
Tarrytown	98
Newark	100
Trenton	99

Part of the explanation for the figures being so close to 99 percent is that the figure obviously must be greater than 95 percent and *any* substantial extension of shelf-time period would approach the 99 percent level. Nevertheless, it was a useful observation that weeding criteria for these five libraries could be developed for the 99 percent level by developing the shelf-time period for the 95 percent level. This information is of special value to libraries using the marked spine method of creating cut-points; it indicates a future date for weeding without a need for monthly counts at circulation to find out when the 99 percent level is reached.

3. The amount of the collection that must be retained to keep that extra 4 percent of the future usage (from 95 percent to 99 percent) requires keeping much more than 4 percent of the collection. A high price is paid in shelf space in the primary areas in order to provide such a relatively small amount of usage.

Percentage of the Collection That Must be Retained
to Keep the Additional 4% of Usage

Morristown	9.1%
Briarcliff	22.2
Tarrytown	22.8
Newark	12.3
Trenton	20.0

The library, depending on its objectives, should seriously consider whether such small additions to future circulation are worth the cost of retaining the additional number of volumes.

In each library there was a shelf-time period at which the percentage of volumes kept became greater than the percentage of future circulation that would be retained. Table 28 and Table 29 show, for example, that in order to increase the future circulation level from 87 percent to 93.1 percent in Morristown, another 11 percent of the collection must be retained. This might be called the most efficient cut-point. Likewise, this most efficient cut-point in Tarrytown is at 69.2 percent, where an additional 11 percent of the collection must be kept in order to achieve 7.8 percent more usage. In practice, this most efficient cut-point could be refined and made more precise. In the first three cases, the 0 month shelf-time period includes this cut-point, and it is impossible to pinpoint it. Only in Newark and Trenton can the ratio change be observed, where at the four month shelf-time period the percentage of use retained is greater than the percentage of the collection that must be retained in the core.

Moving in either direction away from this cut-point, the efficiency increases and decreases rapidly. For instance, in Newark, going from the 49.4 percent to the 61.6 percent level of future use, 13 percent more usage was obtained with 5 percent of the collection, whereas at 99 percent, it required 11.9 percent of the collection to get to the 100 percent level of future usage.

THE VALIDATION STUDIES

Two validation studies were made. The first was to judge whether the core collection identified was, in fact, the part of the collection that circulated. The second was to observe whether weeding had the predicted effect upon circulation. While both of these studies reconfirmed the predictions, it is suggested that a number of additional studies should be undertaken. These

Table 28

INCREASE IN CIRCULATION VS. INCREASE IN COLLECTION

Library	Shelf-Time Period		Usage to be Retained		Increase in Retained Usage	Increase in Core Collection
	From	To	From	To		
Briarcliff	0	1	71.7%	79.0%	7.3%	8.1%
Tarrytown	0	1	69.2	77.0	7.8	11.5
Morristown	0	1	87.0	93.1	6.1	11.0
Trenton	3	4	76.0	79.1	3.1	1.7
	4	5	79.1	80.3	1.2	3.0
Newark	3	4	74.8	77.9	3.1	2.5
	4	5	77.9	80.5	2.6	3.6

Table 29

SHELF-TIME PERIODS OF THE CIRCULATION AND COLLECTION SAMPLES COMPARED (%), DETAILED DATA, FIVE LIBRARIES

Cumulative Shelf-Time Period (Mos.)	Briarcliff Circulation	Briarcliff Collection	Tarrytown Circulation	Tarrytown Collection	Morristown Circulation	Morristown Collection	Trenton Circulation	Trenton Collection	Newark Circulation	Newark Collection
0	71.7	21.7	69.2	23.6	87.0	41.0	51.1	11.9	49.4	14.1
1	79.0	29.8	77.0	34.1	93.1	52.0	64.9	15.9	61.6	19.4
2	84.7	36.8	82.8	41.9	96.8	56.2	69.6	20.0	69.9	22.1
3	86.1	41.0	85.4	46.5	97.6	60.2	76.0	21.8	74.8	26.2
4	90.1	46.7	87.7	50.7	98.4	63.2	79.1	23.5	77.9	28.7
5	94.1	51.8	89.3	54.5	99.2	65.3	80.3	26.5	80.5	32.3
6	95.5	56.4	90.9	58.1	–	68.4	82.3	29.3	83.4	33.5
7	97.2	63.6	92.7	61.1	–	71.0	84.7	30.8	84.4	36.4
8	97.5	67.7	93.5	62.3	–	72.1	85.8	33.2	86.8	38.7
9	97.7	69.9	94.0	65.3	99.5	74.2	87.5	34.9	–	40.5
10	98.3	71.7	94.8	66.9	–	74.9	87.8	37.3	88.1	42.4
11	98.6	73.1	95.0	68.6	–	77.1	89.3	38.8	89.6	45.1
12	–	75.1	95.3	70.9	100.0	77.3	89.9	40.1	90.4	46.9
13	–	76.9	95.6	72.6	–	78.2	–	42.2	91.2	48.7
14	98.9	78.6	–	73.5	–	79.2	90.4	44.0	92.7	51.9
15	–	79.5	–	75.2	–	–	91.3	46.3	93.2	53.8
20	99.7	84.0	97.1	81.5	–	83.8	93.3	52.8	94.5	59.7
25	100.0	88.6	97.9	85.7	–	88.1	95.7	50.5	95.6	63.3
30	–	92.2	98.4	89.3	–	89.5	96.5	61.0	96.9	69.5
35	–	95.1	–	91.4	–	91.8	96.8	62.9	97.7	71.1
40	–	96.3	98.7	93.5	–	93.0	97.4	66.6	99.0	73.1
42	–	–	99.0	93.7	–	–	–	–	–	–
45	–	97.6	99.2	94.5	–	94.6	97.7	69.2	99.5	75.9
50	–	98.8	99.5	96.0	–	95.8	98.3	71.5	–	78.1
55	–	99.6	99.7	96.8	–	96.3	–	72.4	99.7	80.4
60	–	97.7	–	–	–	96.5	–	73.5	–	82.7
65	–	–	100.0	97.3	–	96.7	98.6	73.7	–	85.0
70	–	100.0	–	97.5	–	–	98.9	75.2	100.0	86.3
75	–	–	–	97.7	–	–	–	76.3	–	87.0
100	–	–	–	98.9	–	97.0	99.1	80.4	–	92.0
200	–	–	–	99.8	–	99.8	99.7	91.8	–	98.0
300	–	–	–	100.0	–	100.0	100.0	97.2	–	99.8
400	–	–	–	–	–	–	–	99.1	–	100.0
500	–	–	–	–	–	–	–	99.8	–	–
600 (50 yrs!)	–	–	–	–	–	–	–	100.0	–	–

*This table is summarized by Table 1.

would certainly tend to increase librarians' confidence in the entire weeding concept.

The earlier method of validation was attempted in one of the five libraries, the Tarrytown Library. In this library the predicted and actual figures developed were strikingly similar (see Table 6). The suggested procedure was used to identify a core collection—that is, the shelf-time period cut-off date was established by observing the dates due on the book cards. At the 95 percent level of future use, it was predicted that of 340 circulating volumes, 323 volumes (95 percent) would be from the previously identified core collection, and 17 volumes would not. In other words, at the 95 percent level, 95 percent of the volumes should have the 13 month shelf-time period variable that had been pre-selected.

Approximately seven weeks after the original prediction, a study was made of the book cards retained at the circulation desk over a four-day period. Only complete days, with records intact, were used. The date data was tabulated and reviewed. The question asked was whether or not, based upon the original prediction, a certain circulating volume had been identified as part of the core collection. Table 6 shows the results. Using the core collection previously identified as satisfying 95 percent of the future use, 93.5 percent of the circulation would have been retained. At the 99 percent level, 99.4 percent would have been retained. Both of these figures are well within the statistically expected range for valid prediction.

In the Harrison validation, the fiction collection was weeded, as described elsewhere, and monthly records were made to see what proportion of circulation was represented by the newly weeded collection (see Table 10). In the first six months after weeding, the proportion of fiction circulating *had* increased 6.2 percent. Four months later another study was made, and fiction use represented 48.6 percent of the total circulation, still 3.3 percent higher than the pre-weeded level.

In addition, the adult biography collection was weeded in accordance with this author's instructions. Here, for the first time anywhere, *all* of the books with unmarked spines were weeded out; 32 percent of the total collection was removed. Six weeks later a study was made, and biography had retained the identical proportion of total adult circulation that it had previously enjoyed: 3.4 percent. At least for this library, deep weeding has *not* reduced circulation.

MODELS OF CORE COLLECTIONS

Several attempts by other researchers have been made to describe a useful generalized model for identifying core collections for all libraries. (While used with a somewhat different meaning elsewhere, in this present study the term "model" includes the concept of "an idealized standard for comparison" rather than a mathematical formula needed to produce such a standard.) The value of models would have been in the ability to predict cut-points and the size of core collections in all libraries. Models might also have generalized the results in such a way that they could have been applied to a collection automatically, as long as certain similarities between the model and the collection existed. Unfortunately, no such generalized model was found, nor is it likely to be found. It is a finding of this study that an individual model of a core collection is required for each individual library, and that it can be constructed from the current circulation patterns.

The improbability of finding a useful generalized model stems from two factors: first, because the circulation characteristics of libraries vary so greatly, each library ought to have its own model. None of the libraries observed, prior to a detailed study, could have established with certainty generalized characteristics that could have predicted either a cut-off point or the size of the core collection.

Second, it would appear from informal observation that the model will continually change as the collection is changed to follow each proposed model. For example, when part of the fiction collection was moved to closed stacks in Morristown, the pattern of usage of these volumes changed radically. Thus, if the accessibility and location of a collection affected these models, it is likely that many other variables (including weeding) could influence them also. The implications involved in a changing model seem to reject the existence of a fixed generalized model.

It is proposed that *a valid model would reflect the current use pattern of a library.* If this concept is accepted, then Figure 1 would represent the proposed five models. These models can be applied to weeding a collection by drawing a horizontal line at the level of use one is willing to sacrifice, and then reading the shelf-time period from the bottom axis, where the intersection occurs, which will create that use level. Such a line gives less precision than the tables from which the graph is drawn, so from a practical point of view, the tables are easier and more accurate to use.

The five graphs (Figures 2 through 6) can be used to evaluate the present collection in two ways. First, the closer the lines, the better the collection. In an idealized collection, the shelf-time characteristics of the collection exactly match the shelf-time characteristics of the circulating volumes. This would indicate that all the volumes on the shelves had been used relatively recently.

Second, the graph identifies that *percentage* of the collection *unlikely* to be used at any given predicted level of circulation. The vertical distance to the collection sample line represents the percentage of the volumes likely to receive no future use. The greater the distance between the two lines, along any vertical axis, the greater the number of volumes that will be weeded.

Those models of the collections that chart the imprint date criterion (Figures 7 through 11) give visible evidence that imprint age is an inferior weeding criterion. The closeness of the two lines, compared with the first set of charts, indicates the reduced amount of weeding possible. However, it does show a close relationship to the shelf-time period criterion in that those libraries closely matching the circulation patterns in shelf-time period also match it closely in imprint date.

Notice again, that Tarrytown is a "good" collection and that Trenton is not. Notice also that the predictor of future use (the circulation sample distribution) takes far longer to get to the levels of use that most libraries would prefer.

Figure 1

**CIRCULATION SAMPLES COMPARED—SHELF-TIME PERIODS:
SUGGESTED AS MODELS FOR THE COLLECTION, FIVE LIBRARIES**

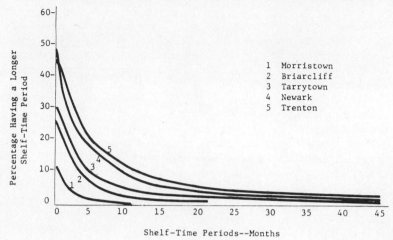

    1 Morristown
    2 Briarcliff
    3 Tarrytown
    4 Newark
    5 Trenton

Shelf-Time Periods--Months

Figure 2

**CIRCULATION AND COLLECTION CHARACTERISTICS
SHELF-TIME PERIODS VERSUS PERCENTAGE REPRESENTED, BRIARCLIFF**

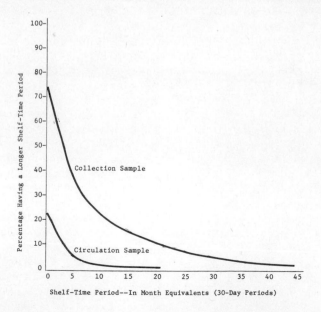

Shelf-Time Period--In Month Equivalents (30-Day Periods)

Figure 3

CIRCULATION AND COLLECTION CHARACTERISTICS
SHELF-TIME PERIODS VERSUS PERCENTAGE REPRESENTED, TARRYTOWN

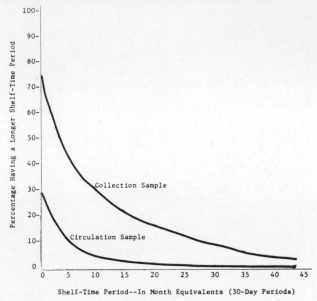

Figure 4

CIRCULATION AND COLLECTION CHARACTERISTICS
SHELF-TIME PERIODS VERSUS PERCENTAGE REPRESENTED, MORRISTOWN

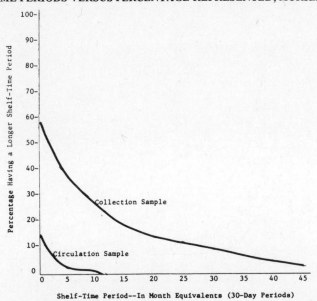

Figure 5

CIRCULATION AND COLLECTION CHARACTERISTICS
SHELF-TIME PERIODS VERSUS PERCENTAGE REPRESENTED, TRENTON

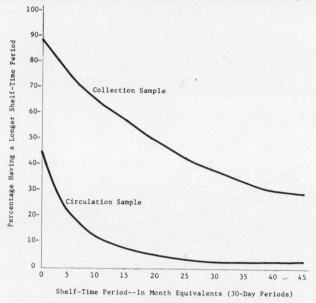

Shelf-Time Period--In Month Equivalents (30-Day Periods)

Figure 6

CIRCULATION AND COLLECTION CHARACTERISTICS
SHELF-TIME PERIODS VERSUS PERCENTAGE REPRESENTED, NEWARK

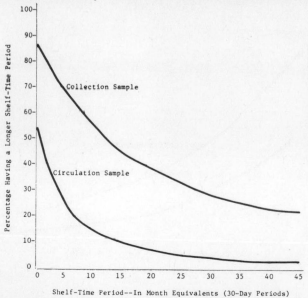

Shelf-Time Period--In Month Equivalents (30-Day Periods)

Figure 7

**PERCENTAGE OF CIRCULATION SAMPLE AND COLLECTION SAMPLE
OVER Y YEARS IN AGE VERSUS AGE OF BOOKS IN YEARS,
BRIARCLIFF**

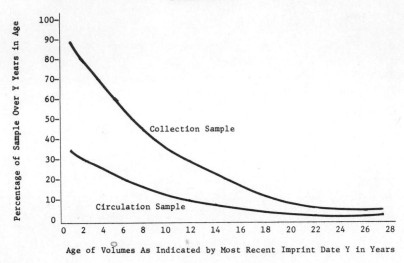

Age of Volumes As Indicated by Most Recent Imprint Date Y in Years

Figure 8

**PERCENTAGE OF CIRCULATION SAMPLE AND COLLECTION SAMPLE
OVER Y YEARS IN AGE VERSUS AGE OF BOOKS IN YEARS,
TARRYTOWN**

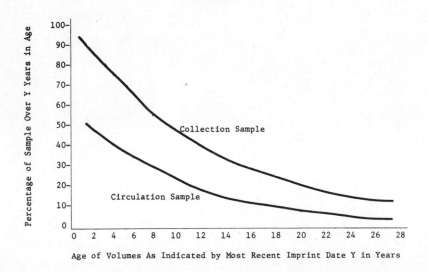

Age of Volumes As Indicated by Most Recent Imprint Date Y in Years

Figure 9

**PERCENTAGE OF CIRCULATION SAMPLE AND COLLECTION SAMPLE
OVER Y YEARS IN AGE VERSUS AGE OF BOOKS IN YEARS,
MORRISTOWN**

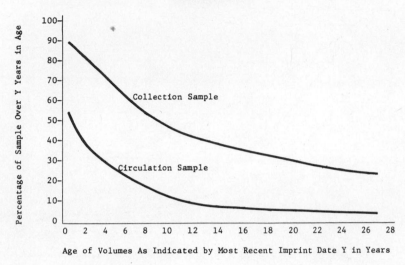

Age of Volumes As Indicated by Most Recent Imprint Date Y in Years

Figure 10

**PERCENTAGE OF CIRCULATION SAMPLE AND COLLECTION SAMPLE
OVER Y YEARS IN AGE VERSUS AGE OF BOOKS IN YEARS,
TRENTON**

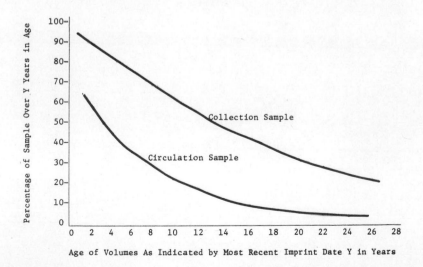

Age of Volumes As Indicated by Most Recent Imprint Date Y in Years

Figure 11

PERCENTAGE OF CIRCULATION SAMPLE AND COLLECTION SAMPLE
OVER Y YEARS IN AGE VERSUS AGE OF BOOKS IN YEARS, NEWARK

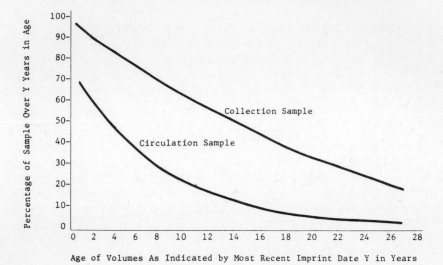

Age of Volumes As Indicated by Most Recent Imprint Date Y in Years

APPENDIX B

DETAILED METHODOLOGY AND PROBLEMS IN CREATING SHELF-TIME PERIOD IN THE FIVE LIBRARIES

THE METHODOLOGY

The basic method used in this study, called the current circulation method, involved recording the complete adult fiction circulation of several consecutive days. The book cards removed from circulating volumes at the circulation desks were examined. The days studied were then used to represent the entire circulation pattern of fiction (i.e., these days constituted a sample). Prediction of future use was based on the distribution of the variables: the shelf-time period and the most recent imprint date.

The number of days for which the data was collected was determined by the size of the sample required. Thus, if fifty fiction volumes were circulated per day, and 400 samples were needed, eight days of circulation were employed. In each library an attempt was made to use days when no special activities were going on, and to include at least one Saturday. However, in all cases, consecutive days were used, to prevent the over-representation of any one day in the week.

Finally, since only complete days were tabulated, it was necessary to use days in which no book cards had been removed from the records and reslipped into returned books. Libraries were requested to delay reslipping until after the sample was taken. Only the previous two or three days of circulation were examined on each visit to a library, so that unslipped, returned volumes would not accumulate and become a storage problem for the libraries.

In addition to the method described above, the historic reconstruction method (modified) was employed in one library. This method would ideally record the entire usage history of each volume in a collection, identifying the most frequently used volumes which account for 95 percent and 99 percent of the total use, and describing these volumes in terms of the selected variables. The methodology was modified with the objective of reconstructing the most recent three years of use.

For each volume in the sample, the number of uses, as indicated on the book card, was recorded for each of the most recent three years. When the complete information for three years was not available, the indicated rate of usage over a shorter time period was assumed to have occurred over the entire

141

three-year period. This procedure was used only once and was considered a subordinate part of the entire study.

The Data Collected. The following data, when available, was recorded for each volume in each sample (see Exhibit 1, page 143 for form used):

1.   The most recent imprint date of a volume.
2.   The three most recent dates on the book cards.
3.   The total number of circulations for each of the last three years.
4.   Miscellaneous information, including the loan period, location of volumes in closed stacks, whether the book was part of the McNaughton Collection, and the date the volume was borrowed, if in circulation.

Description of the Collection. All parts of the fiction collection were considered in the sampling. First, the most obvious part consisted of the books on the open shelves. Second, cards for all of the books in circulation were sampled. These were considered on exactly the same basis as the books on the shelves. Third, there were books in a variety of locations. These included books in closed stacks, not accessible to the reader for browsing; books in special locations because they were new, of special interest, or parts of the McNaughton Collection; books in special displays; books on reserve shelves; books being processed; books being returned to the shelves; books being rebound or repaired.

Whenever practical, these books were considered to be in one straight run, in a predetermined order (see page 145—Instructions for Data Collections). A systematic sample was taken of each collection. In examining the collection, the volumes of book cards were physically removed, studied, and then returned to their former location. The sample was selected by including every xth volume (say every 50th volume). Certain rules were made for counting the volumes for the purpose of selecting the samples. Counting was from left to right, front to back (when books were shelved two deep), and top to bottom. Books located on top of other books were counted first. Wherever books were in such disarray that no logical order was apparent, arbitrary ordering took place.

In order that systematic errors could be identified, the sampling was done in two halves. In each half of the sample, the first volume counted was determined by a number taken from a random number table, and each set of books was removed separately. The two halves of the sample were compared and combined. In this check for hidden periodicities in the data no serious differences between the two halves of the systematic sample were found.

Table 30 shows the results and data for both halves of the collection sample. The maximum variations were all well below the expected figures that would have indicated a systematic error.

Exhibit 1
DATA SHEET

LIBRARY:
SAMPLE METHOD:
SAMPLE SOURCE:

DATE:

STUDY #:

Sample No.	Last Imprint Date	Dates on Book Cards			Number of Circulations			Notes
		3rd	2nd	1st	Year to			
		Most Recent			/ /67	/ /68	/ /69	
1								
2								
3								
4								
5								
6								
7								
8								
9								
10								
11								
12								
13								
etc								

Table 30

THE TOTAL COLLECTION SAMPLE COMPARED WITH ITS TWO HALVES
VARIABLE: SHELF-TIME PERIOD, FIVE LIBRARIES

Percent of the Total Collection Predicted to be in the Core Collection--keeping approximately 99% of the current use	Briarcliff	Tarrytown	Morristown	Trenton	Newark
Predicted by total sample	78.6	94.5	65.3	75.2	73.6
Predicted by the 1st sampling run through	78.4	94.6	64.1	77.8	75.1
Predicted by the 2nd sampling run through.	78.7	94.5	66.7	72.4	72.3
Maximum variation of the parts from the whole sample	0.2	0.1	1.4	2.8	1.5
Percent of the Total Collection Predicted to be in the Core Collection--keeping approximately 95% of the current use					
Predicted by total sample	56.4	70.9	56.2	55.2	61.3
Predicted by the 1st sampling run through	55.0	70.4	53.9	57.2	63.7
Predicted by the 2nd sampling run through	57.9	71.1	58.6	52.9	58.7
Maximum variation of the parts from the whole sample	1.5	0.5	2.6	2.3	2.6

INSTRUCTIONS FOR DATA COLLECTORS

1. Fill out the heading carefully and check with me before starting your work.

2. **Last Imprint Date.** Enter the most recent printed date recorded in the book. This might be the copyright date, or the edition date.

3. **Dates on the Book Card.** Enter the three most recent dates that can be found on the book card, which would indicate three successive uses. It might be necessary to look at all four printing positions on the card, as cards are often not stamped in order. Dates are to be recorded by number (i.e., 3/17/69). Remember this list:

Jan. 1	July 7
Feb. 2	Aug. 8
Mar. 3	Sept. 9
Apr. 4	Oct. 10
May 5	Nov. 11
June 6	Dec. 12

a) Where information does not exist, enter a dash.

b) If illegible, call me for help.

4. **Number of Circulations.** Count the number of circulations for each of the last twelve-month periods.

year to / /67
year to / /68
year to / /69

a) When the use record starts in one of these periods, enter the date of the first entry (e.g., 4/4/68).

b) Look at all four sections of the book card for the information.

5. Under NOTES, use these abbreviations, and make sure the data is entered for each volume.

ND   =   no data
OE   =   one entry
OD   =   overdue (show where with *)

7
14
21   =   shows length of the loan period on that volume
28

MC   =   McNaughton Collection
MY   =   mysteries

6. **Sample Source.** From shelves, circulation desk, a new book rack, closed shelves or rooms, McNaughton Collection.

7. When data is not available, get imprint date from card catalog or shelf list, at the time data is being recorded.

8. When pulling books or cards from the shelves or elsewhere, keep them in alphabetical order (original order) and mark location from which they came with a 3" x 5" card so that books may be reshelved or cards refiled easily.

9. Initial each page.

10. Follow order of books for sampling.

a)	Main shelves	e)	Overdues
b)	Current fiction	f)	Reservations
c)	Paperbacks	g)	In process books, slipped
d)	Circulation files		

--- --- ---

Source of Certain Data. Most of the data in the study came from the volume itself or from its book card. When the volume was in circulation and the book card lacked the information, data (such as the imprint date) was taken from the cards in the shelf-list or from the public catalog. Other data, such as the loan period, came from special markings on the dust jacket, on the book itself, or on the book cards.

Some Possible Distortions. It was noticed that a number of things might possibly affect the circulation of the books. Two of the sample libraries had closed-shelf arrangements for many of their volumes (4,500 in Trenton; 1,500 in Morristown). A sampling of these titles showed extremely light usage of these volumes (Table 31). Multiple locations for similar volumes and special displays were not uncommon and could have affected use. The use or non-use of a reserve system also might have affected circulation.

Validation Study. Approximately seven weeks after a prediction was made based upon the initial sample, a study was made of the cards at the circulation desk of the Tarrytown Public Library over a four-day period. Only complete days, with records intact, were used. All book cards were used in this study if they had one or more dates on them indicating their existence in the collection at the time of the first study. Each card was studied and its characteristics noted and tabulated as to whether, based upon the original prediction, it would have been considered part of the core collection.

Shelf-Time Periods. In determining shelf-time period, two distinguishable measurements were included in the term. The first, open-end shelf-time period, described the characteristics of the whole collection; this was the elapsed time between the last use of a book and the date of the study. It measured the most recent length of time in which no use had been made of the volume.

The closed-end shelf-time period related to the time period between the last two uses of a volume. This measurement was used in the predictor part of the study, which looked at the circulation sample. With the book in circulation, the shelf-time period (terminated by the current withdrawal) was measured from the book card.

Measurement of Shelf-Time Periods. Since the date a book was *returned* to the library was not recorded, no direct readings could be made to determine

Table 31

COMPARISON OF CLOSED STACK AND OPEN SHELF COLLECTIONS
IN RELATIONSHIP TO BOOK USE, MORRISTOWN

	Closed Stacks	Open Shelves	Total Collection
In the probable use range (100% at 12 mo. shelf-time period)	39.0%	81.4%	77.3%
As above but adding insufficient data samples to weeded collection	18.4	79.7	69.0
Insufficient imprint date data	26.3	2.3	6.7
Insufficient shelf-time period data	49.4	2.0	10.7
Number of volumes in collections	1512	7236	8748
Number of samples	87	391	478
Number with unusable imprint date data	23	9	32
Number with unusable shelf-time period date	43	8	51

shelf-time period. For example, if a 28-day book was borrowed on July 2, it was due July 30, and the book card would have been so marked. When such a book on the shelves was examined at a later date, it was not known if it was returned on July 2, the date borrowed, or *any other* subsequent date. For the sake of consistency, several rules were created:

1. The average time a book remained out on loan was computed by taking a sample in each library. This was done by averaging the circulation time of approximately 100 volumes as they were returned to the loan desk.

Table 32 shows that in Briarcliff, for example, the average volume with a one-week loan period was retained by the reader for eight days. In Newark, using two- and four-week loan periods considered together, it was found that the average volume was retained seventeen days.

Table 32

NUMBER OF DAYS THE AVERAGE CIRCULATING VOLUME
WAS RETAINED BY THE CLIENT, FIVE LIBRARIES

Official Loan Period	Briarcliff	Tarrytown	Morristown	Trenton	Newark
1 week	8 days		6 days		
2 weeks	11 days	10 days		12 days	
3 weeks	19 days		19 days		17 days (combined
4 weeks		20 days		26 days	average)

2. The loan period was subtracted from the date due, and the figure found in Item no. 1 above was added to it. This produced the best estimate of the day a book was returned to the library, and it was used to compute shelf-time period. For example, if a volume contained a date due of July 30 and had a two-week loan period, the computation was as follows:

Date due	July 30
Subtract loan period	14
	—
Date borrowed	16
Add days in Briarcliff circulation	11
	—
Date returned to shelf	27

Thus, a volume with a July 30 due date was assumed to be back in the library and shelved on July 27, and this was the date utilized in computing its shelf-time period.

3. In order to insure consistency and simplify the identification of shelf-time period, a table was constructed similar to Table 33, locating each date in its proper cell; this table was used for assigning books to their shelf-time period cells. Each table was valid for use for only one specific date.

4. To compute the collection sample, each volume was treated as if it had been circulated on the day of the study. Thus, if a volume on the shelves on April 30 had the most recent due date of April 8 (1969), it was assigned to the one-month shelf-time period cell (Table 33). This is a minimum shelf-time period, since the volume may continue to remain on the shelf unused for a much longer time before it actually circulates again.

Table 33

TABLE USED TO ASSIGN BOOKS TO SHELF-TIME PERIOD CELLS,
ADJUSTING BOOK CARD DATE DUE FOR AVERAGE TIME
BOOK CIRCULATES AND FOR LOAN PERIOD

Usable April 30, 1969 Only

Briarcliff Library

No. of Days on Shelf	Shelf-Time Period	28-Day Books Dates Included	7-Day Books Dates Included
0-30	0	4/9/69 - 5/28/69	3/30/69 - 5/7/69
31-60	1	3/10/69 - 4/8/69	3/1/69 - 3/29/69
61-90	2	2/8/69 - 3/9/69	1/30/69 - 2/28/69
91-120	3	1/9/69 - 2/7/69	12/31/68 - 1/29/69
121-150	4	12/10/68 - 1/8/69	12/1/68 - 12/30/68
151-180	5	11/10/68 - 12/9/68	11/1/68 - 11/30/68
181-210	6	10/11/68 - 11/9/68	10/2/68 - 10/31/68
211-240	7	9/11/68 - 10/10/68	9/2/68 - 10/1/68
241-270	8	8/12/68 - 9/10/68	3/3/68 - 9/1/68
271-300	9	7/13/68 - 8/11/68	7/4/68 - 8/2/68
301-330	10	6/13/68 - 7/12/68	6/4/68 - 7/3/68
331-360	11	5/14/68 - 6/12/68	5/5/68 - 6/3/68
361-390	12	4/14/68 - 5/13/68	4/5/68 - 5/4/68
391-420	13	3/15/68 - 4/13/68	3/6/68 - 4/4/68
421-450	14	2/14/68 - 3/14/68	2/5/68 - 3/5/68
451-480	15	1/15/68 - 2/13/68	1/6/68 - 2/4/68
481-510	16	12/16/67 - 1/14/68	12/7/67 - 1/5/68
511-540	17	11/16/67 - 12/15/67	11/7/67 - 12/6/67
541-570	18	10/17/67 - 11/15/67	10/8/67 - 11/6/67
571-600	19	9/17/67 - 10/16/67	9/8/67 - 10/7/67

The cells called "months" were thirty-day periods, not calendar months. The "zero" month represented any computed time less than thirty-one days. This cell might have built into it some inconsistency as it related to the rest of the cells. The reason for this was that aside from any formula used to determine shelf-time periods, there was often more information available for the zero cell.

For example, if a book had June 10 and June 11 recorded, there was no point in applying any formula. That book was taken out, returned within one day, and taken out again. Therefore, it was put in the zero shelf-time period cell.

The computation might have produced a minus fourteen figure, and negative shelf-time periods were impossible. Therefore, whenever a minus figure was indicated, that book went into cell 0-30, or the zero cell.

Some situations might have created errors in assigning a volume to a specific cell. When the normal date due for a book fell on a day that the library would be closed, the date due used was the next date on which the library would be open. This meant that knowing the loan period for any given volume did not guarantee that the date it was borrowed could be ascertained.

Another problem existed with overdue books, since the book card kept no clear record of the date that the book was returned. In those cases, an overdue book just returned to the library might now show a long shelf-time period, when in reality, it had a short one.

SOME PROBLEMS WITH SHELF-TIME PERIODS

The First Shelf-Time Period. The first shelf-time period was the length of time a book remained on the shelf before its first use. This time period could be reconstructed if the book's shelving date were recorded, but this was usually not indicated. Therefore, there was no acceptable method for finding the first shelf-time period, and samples omitted from the study because of "no data" might actually have had very long shelf-time periods.

Missing Data. Data that would have been of interest in this study was often missing on the book cards. This was to be expected, since the book card is used to *control* circulation, whereas the study attempted to *recreate* circulation data. Several factors contributed to this lack of data.

1. *Used-Up Cards.* It was the custom in all of the sample libraries to discard cards that had no room for further entries or that were too worn to work properly in a charging machine. Since the cards of the most-used books were used up the fastest, they were the most likely to have incomplete information.

2. *Blank Cards.* In every sample there were some instances when no use data at all was available on the book card, since the book cards were undated. Very old books, apparently unused, often had cards that were blank. Rebound books of various ages commonly received new blank cards when the books were rebound. At the time of the study, these were often still blank. Similarly, charge-out systems were occasionally changed, and new cards were systematically placed in a major part of the collection. In two of the sample libraries, this had occurred when the system was switched from hand dating to machine dating.

A reasonable solution for the future is for the library to go through the entire collection, dating blank cards with the current date. Whenever cards are replaced, the date of last use should be carried forward to the new card.

Mechanical Problems.

1. A number of cards were illegible, had multiple stamping of the same date in different locations, and were not dated in chronological order. This may have caused some error in determining shelf-time periods. In an attempt to avoid errors, items for which the information was not clear were not used in the study.

2. Perhaps a related series of problems were caused by the overdue books, stolen books, or lost book cards. When book cards were lost, the necessary information was lost, and there was no way to evaluate such losses in the study. The same is true of stolen books.

3. The length of the shelf-time period cells created another problem. A number of decisions were made through trial and error. It was originally thought that shelf-time periods should be measured in years, a period used in some other library studies. It was soon apparent that the conclusions from such an approach would not be very helpful, since in the first pilot study 99 percent of the usage occurred with books having a one-year (or shorter) shelf-time period, and 100 percent having a two-year (or shorter) shelf-time period.

The next attempt was to use calendar months. This was discarded because it resulted in cells of unequal duration. Also considered (and discarded) was the use of weeks or days as cells. Next, fixed months of twenty-eight days or thirty days were tried. It was finally decided that thirty-day periods would best represent a standardized month.

Which Shelf-Time Period to Use as a Predictor. Field experiments were used in the search for a meaningful shelf-time period. It was first reasoned that the longest recorded shelf-time period for each volume might be useful as the variable. Aside from the mechanical problem of looking at numerous entries (which were not always in chronological order) on several thousand cards, there were other considerations that figured in the decision to use no more than the last two dates for the principal data.

First, it seemed likely that the latest information would reflect the *present* patterns of circulation. Currency of information seemed a valuable ideal. Second, the study showed that the addition of earlier shelf-time periods did not improve the prediction. Finally, the further back one went, the less complete was the information, which in itself might well have distorted any of the findings.

SOME PROBLEMS IN THE SAMPLING

Books at the Bindery. In every library studied, a certain number of the books still in the active collection had been temporarily withdrawn because they were damaged. These were in various stages of processing and repair. Sometimes minor repairs were made within the library itself, other times the volumes were rebound by outside contractors.

Occasionally book card records were retained for such volumes, but often new blank cards were issued. Information from such volumes was either distorted, incomplete, or non-existent. In no case were these books used for the sample.

Books in Locked Cases. Generally omitted from the sample were small quantities of books in locked shelves, closets, or offices, which were not readily accessible to the public. They were omitted primarily because their number was small (three libraries had virtually none), but also because these books had substantially reduced usage.

Two of the libraries, however, had substantial parts of their collection stored in closed stack areas. Because of the large number of volumes involved, these books were considered parts of the regular collection and were included in the sample.

Some books not considered in the study were volumes semi-permanently stored in the director's office or in the office of some other library employee. Some were on library science topics, but others were new volumes that the librarian wanted to peruse before shelving them.

Branch Libraries and Deposit Collections. All of the libraries studied had current or old deposit collections, usually in schools. The three largest libraries had branches. In each case, only the collection housed at the main library was studied.

Renewals. The libraries used a range of techniques for handling renewals, even though most of them did not officially permit them. The effect of renewals was not isolated in this study. Whenever a renewal occurred, a new entry was made on the book card and it was treated as a new transaction.

Changes in the Loan Periods. Each of the libraries had more than one type of loan period. Shorter loan periods were generally extended as books received less use. While many of the books showed that a loan period had been altered, none showed *when* the change had been made. For the purpose of this study, the current loan period was used in computing shelf-time.

Summer Loans. Several of the libraries made loans for periods of two months or more. No *special* record was made of this transaction, and such distortion as might have been introduced by this procedure was disregarded.

Partial Data. Wherever partial data existed, as much of it as possible was used. For instance, imprint age might be available, while dates for computing shelf-time period might be lacking.

Systematic Sample Problem. One of the problems in selecting books for the sample was that the sample was taken while the library was operating. Since the study included taking a systematic sample (every 20th volume, for instance), it is likely that the users' removal of volumes from the shelves during the sampling somewhat distorted the results of the study. However, there is no evidence that the results would have been significantly different if there had been no user activity during the period of data-gathering.

Another problem occurred during the sampling. Two independent samples were taken for each collection and compared to see if any regular distortion could be uncovered. This meant going through the collection twice. For example, the first sample might have examined the seventh volume and then every 20th volume after that, while the second sampling might have started with the 15th volume, followed by every 20th volume after that.

The usual procedure was that each book was brought to a desk, the data was tabulated, and then the volume was replaced by the same person who removed it. In the first library sampled, some books were being examined while a second book-gatherer was counting and removing his books. This caused an overlap of book selection from the shelves, for the second book-gatherer counted every 20th volume *after* the first sample had already been removed and was still off the shelves. Actually, even though this destroyed the plan of the systematic sampling, it did not seem to affect the results. In all later studies, the procedure consisted of replacing the first sample before removing the second sample.

Method of Finding the Imprint Date. Several methods were used to find the imprint date, depending on the availability of the book itself. If the book was available, then both the verso and the recto of the title page were examined for the date. In several cases, when the date was not included, the book was omitted from the sample.

If the book was not available (i.e., if it was circulating), then the book card was examined. When the imprint date was not on the card (only Newark and the McNaughton book cards showed this date), a search was made in the shelf-list or the public catalog. Often such a search failed to reveal imprint date and the volume was excluded from the sample.

The variable "most recent imprint date" was always recorded in terms of chronological years (i.e., 1968, 1967, etc.). This meant that 1969 (the year of the study) was an incomplete year, and did not parallel other imprint years. It also meant that for each library the size of this first cell, 1969, was different from each other library, since no two studies were done on the same day.

McNaughton Collection Problems. Because the McNaughton Collection represented such a large percentage of the usage in three libraries that subscribed to it, a summary was made of its special characteristics. In all three libraries, this collection was segregated from the rest of the collection. The McNaughton Collection was rented from the Bro-Dart Company for a regular monthly fee. Books came preprocessed. All three of the libraries permitted usage of the collection without special charges. Each month, one-tenth of the books could be returned to Bro-Dart in exchange for new selections. It was the most current fiction collection in the library. In each of the libraries, those volumes that were considered to be of permanent interest were purchased.

Multiple Copies. A previous, informal study attempted to treat all copies of the same title together and to record their combined use pattern as if dealing with one volume. From many points of view this proved to be impractical.

It was difficult to identify multiple copies without an examination of the shelf-list. Even when multiple copies were identified, however, finding the books proved to be difficult. They might have been in any of several locations: out in circulation, in reserves, misshelved, or in a special location. Since none of the libraries had up-to-date inventories or shelf-lists, the gradual loss of listed volumes made advance identification impossible.

A further problem was imposed by the controls at the circulation desk. Book cards were usually filed according to dates, either borrowed or due, so that it was necessary to examine as many as 24 separate decks of cards in order to find a record of a title.

Finally, even if identical titles were in hand, combining them added a number of problems: the treatment of different imprints, the measurement of shelf-time periods, information missing in some of the volumes. It was decided that each volume was to be handled and considered independently, even if duplicate volumes existed.

APPENDIX C

STATISTICAL METHODOLOGY IN THE
FIVE LIBRARY STUDY

DETERMINATION OF SAMPLE SIZE

The objective of the basic statistical methodology used in this study was to answer the question: "How well does the sample reflect the population from which it was drawn?" This was further divided into two questions:

1. What size sample must be drawn to produce a specified precision (in terms of confidence intervals) in estimates of population proportions? Or how accurate are the predictions, in view of the limitations caused by the number of samples used?

2. Once the specific sample has been drawn, what is the statistically indicated confidence interval for the population proportions?

The following formula was applied to answer the first question on the determination of sample size:

$$n = \frac{4P(1-P)}{E}$$

Where: E = Amount of precision desired in the estimate (one-half the width of the desired confidence interval)

P = Proportion to be estimated

n = Number of samples

Three aspects of using this formula might be noted:

1. The formula assumes a sampling procedure that would produce results similar to a random sample.

2. The size of the population had a negligible effect on the results when the population is large relative to the size of the sample.

3. The 95 percent level of confidence (95 times out of 100 the true proportion will be covered by the computed confidence interval) was accepted

as satisfactory.

When 99 percent of the future use was to be retained (giving a proportion of 99/1), 400 samples were required to produce a confidence interval of 1 percent. This meant that between 98 percent and 100 percent of the future usage should be predicted with a sample size of 400.

Similarly, it was found that at the 95 percent level of future use, 400 samples gave a confidence interval of 2 percent.

Further, at the 50/50 proportion (applicable in estimating the size of a core collection), 400 samples gave a confidence interval of ±5 percent. Since 50/50 gives the largest confidence interval, this is the largest interval possible when the sample size is 400.

For the purposes of this study, the above confidence intervals were accepted as being adequate. Therefore, it was predetermined that samples of approximately 400 would be taken. In practice, because of difficulties or errors made in predicting the number of usable samples, actual samples ranged from 353 to 694 (see Table 5). Table 34 reports the actual computed intervals for each sample.

These intervals (Question 2, page 154) were computed by the formula:

$$p - 1.96 \frac{P\ (1-p)}{n} < P < p + 1.96 \frac{P\ (1-p)}{n}$$

Where: P = Proportion to be estimated

p = Observed proportion

PRACTICAL MEANING OF THE DATA

Some interpretation would be helpful in explaining the practical meaning of this statistical data.

The characteristics reported in Table 5 are: the number of sample volumes actually looked at, and the number of volumes that could be used as valid, meaningful samples. In Briarcliff, for example, 404 samples were taken at the circulation desk. When the book cards were observed, only 353 of these samples included enough information to determine shelf-time period. This meant that 51 cards gave no indication that a volume circulating at the time of the sample had had any previous use. The conclusion to be drawn from this is that if 400 useful samples are desired, then perhaps 450 to 500 samples should be taken.

The same problem existed to a lesser degree for the imprint date. In the case of Briarcliff, only ten volumes created an unsolvable problem and could not be used in the sample.

The reason for the variation in the number of volumes in the samples at circulation is that complete days of circulation were taken. In each case, on the

Table 34

SHOWING HOW CLOSELY THE SAMPLES REPRESENT THE
POPULATION—CONFIDENCE INTERVALS AT THE 95% CONFIDENCE LEVEL
FIVE LIBRARIES

Circulation Sample-- Shelf-Time Period	Briarcliff	Tarrytown	Morristown	Trenton	Newark
Predicted use level	98.9%	99.2%	99.2%	98.9%	99.0%
Confidence interval of prediction	±.011	±.010	±.009	±.011	±.010
Predicted use level	95.5	95.0	96.8	95.1	95.1
Confidence interval of prediction	±.024	±.022	±.018	±.023	±.022
Collection Sample-- Shelf-Time Period					
Predicted size of core collection-- percent of total collection--at use level	78.6%	94.5%	65.3%	75.2%	73.6%
Above confidence interval of prediction	±.032	±.021	±.046	±.040	±.042
Predicted size of core collection-- percent of total collection--at use level	56.4	70.9	56.2	55.2	61.3
Above confidence interval of prediction	±.038	±.042	±.048	±.046	±.046

day that the 400th sample was observed, the sampling was stopped. Only in
Trenton, where other problems existed, were fewer than 400 taken.

The number of samples observed in the collection was greater than the
number of samples at circulation because it was easy to get a larger sample from
the collection. This could be done in one day, while circulation sampling took
several days.

First, the number of volumes in the collection was estimated, and then a
systematic sample was taken with every "xth" (say, 10th) volume being
observed. Briarcliff had 708 samples because an error was made in interpreting
that "x."

Table 34 can be interpreted as follows: for Newark, when predicting that
99 percent of the future usage will be retained, the confidence interval is

1 percent. This means that if all volumes in the core collection (as described by the shelf-time period criterion) are retained, then between 98 percent and 100 percent of the future use will be retained 95 percent of the time.

If the study has predicted that using a given cut-point will retain (as in Briarcliff) 56.4 percent of the collection, the collection retained might vary by plus or minus 3.8 percent. In other words, the size of the core collection is likely to be between 59.2 percent and 52.6 percent of the present collection. This will happen nineteen out of twenty times (95 percent of the time). These ranges are caused by the likely error due to the fact that the weeder has looked at the sample and not at the whole population. If the entire collection were observed, the exact size of the core collection could be predicted.

To the degree discussed above, the predictions are likely to miss the exact mark. As with all predictions, they *could* miss the mark by substantially larger amounts.

APPENDIX D

THE STUDY OF THE
HARRISON PUBLIC LIBRARY–PROBLEMS

As has been stated in Chapter 11, the Harrison study was a more practical approach to the problem of weeding. It was designed basically to put to practical use the findings of previous studies, but it was also an attempt to uncover the real problems encountered in an actual weeding situation. The earlier experiments were designed for libraries that had book cards. This study provided an opportunity to create the data needed when such data is not readily available. The Harrison study, because of its value to practical weeding and the fact that it has not been previously reported, is presented here in considerable detail. The collection has been partially weeded by this method, and the resultant impact on circulation and on the collection were reported earlier.

PROBLEMS

Several problems arose during the attempt to establish a shelf-time period mechanically. The steps taken were an attempt to overcome some of these problems. A brief discussion of some of these problems will perhaps forewarn others who may wish to undertake a similar project.

As might have been anticipated, there was no way to guarantee either that the red dots would be applied to every book being circulated or that once applied they would remain on. No completely successful solution to the problem of undotted circulating books was ever reached. Some books circulated and were not dotted. The problem of dots being removed or falling off was handled by instituting a number of other procedures.

Several months after the start of the project, an additional dot was added to every dotted book on the shelves. It was felt that this would solve the problem of dots accidentally falling off since it was unlikely that both would fall off at the same time. Because of the ever-present problem of human error in applying dots, weeded volumes were not discarded but were sent to a branch library. This solution was "safe," but it also violated the entire concept and purpose of the weeding activity.

In the Harrison Library, when actual weeding took place, another compromise was worked out. All volumes that librarians thought should be left in the core collection were retained, including 25 percent of the non-core fiction volumes. A further study showed that this non-core collection had little value, and that the volumes should not have been retained.

As an indication of exactly how the error in applying dots affects statistics, consider the following. When the six-month records of the Harrison Library were compiled (November 1972), it was estimated that approximately 1,000 books that should have been dotted were, in fact, not dotted—an average of over 150 books a month. While this represented a shortage of only 1½ percent a month of the circulating books, it meant that 10 percent of the undotted books being brought to the circulation desk were not being dotted.

Other problems arose. The red dots were not easily visible on a book with an overall red cover. Two solutions were suggested, but not tried. One was that dots be applied in exactly the same place on the spine of each volume—for example, one inch from the bottom. This consistency would make identification easier. The second solution proposed was to have two sets of dots, and to use a different color on the red books.

A final problem was identified in statistical distortions caused by circulation of books with irregular or unusual use patterns. Overdues are one example. A book many months overdue and returned in the first month of the observations would be inaccurately recorded as having a one-month shelf-time period. Interlibrary loan also affects statistics. These books go completely unrecorded, since the physical book is removed from the library. Stolen or lost books have the same distorting effect. All of these examples obscure information that the weeder needs in order to make his decisions.

FINDINGS

Some of the findings were subjective and reflected informal observations made while the experiment was under way. Some came from the staff and users. Still other observations were statistical and controlled. All, however, might be found useful by librarians who want to use this technique.

The experiment caused considerable comment from the patrons. It became clear that some explanation was necessary if the reference department was not to spend all of its time answering questions about the red dots. At first, signs were put up reading "The Mystery of the Red Dot," with no explanation—which generated much interest! Later, an article explaining the study was written for the local newspaper. Since this library was pressed for space and unable to expand quickly enough to house the books already owned, weeding seemed to have a good public relations aspect and to impress the citizens as a very reasonable approach. It became apparent that any weeding experiment should be explained to the library's users in detail.

The experiment was successful. It was apparent from this study that spine marking will develop reasonably accurate indications of the core collection which can satisfy 95 percent of the future use of the library. While it was still underway after sixteen months, it took successively less and less work. Each month, with one exception, more and more of the books being circulated already had the dots on them. In the first month all of the adult volumes circulating had to be dotted, which entailed a rather substantial effort. In the third month, 75 percent of the books circulating already had dots on them and only 25 percent had to be dotted. By the sixth month, only 10 percent needed dots. Thus, as it developed, the work became less burdensome.

One mark of its success was the similarity of the results to the results of the earlier experiment. A look at Table 9 will show the development of patterns very similar to those of the other libraries. The data was not identical, but it reconfirmed the conclusion that each library is a unique institution with its own shelf-time period characteristics.

When only book cards were studied, as in the earlier study, each monthly shelf-time period had to show a larger percentage of circulation, since it was a cumulative figure of what was occurring at one period of time. Each month's figure was added to the next. In this experiment, true circulation figures were actually reported at monthly intervals. This caused erratic figures for Harrison.

One finding was that a somewhat different collection circulated in the summer than in the winter. August, September, and October showed an even pulsation, probably caused by this summer variation. Theoretically, it seems possible that a class that had not circulated before might circulate according to a season or a special event.

The trend is apparent when, in adult fiction, the previously used fiction went from 97 percent in September to only 84 percent in October (see Table 7). It must be added that part of this might have been a statistical problem in which too few samples were taken in September. The size of the sample was increased starting with the October figures.

The length of time the study took points up two characteristics. The first was that the experiment might go on for years, as in academic libraries, where a satisfactory shelf-time period might be five years, or even longer. It would mean a five-year period of applying dots. Alternate methods, such as automatic dotting by charging machines, might improve the quality of such long-term experiments.

The second characteristic recognized as a result of the study's length was that weeding must be done immediately if the maximum number of books are to be weeded. Otherwise, some of the non-core collection gets used, dotted, and preserved as part of the core collection.

One of the purposes of this study was to validate the assumption that different classes of books show different shelf-time period characteristics. The experiment hoped to determine the significance of this difference from a practical point of view. As the experiment unfolded, trends became apparent. In the adult non-fiction collection, *where a significant number of samples were observed*, the practical differences did not seem significant. However, other classes proved to have more significant practical differences.

Depending on the objectives of the weeding, the differences may not be important to the library. If one is attempting to keep 95 percent of the future use of the present collection, one may weed each class when circulation data indicate the 95 percent keeping level has been reached. This would mean weeding one class at a time, which is a reasonable method of weeding. It would require additional control and record keeping, since the books being circulated would have to be recorded by class. This technique would assure a likelihood that *each class* of books in the library would satisfy about 95 percent of the future use now occurring. If the library waited until 95 percent of *all the volumes* coming to circulation were dotted, it would be reasonably certain to satisfy 95 percent of the future use, but this would be only an average of the entire collection. What might be reflected in reality is a higher percentage than 95 percent in one class and a lower than 95 percent in another. However, the second method of weeding is easier to control and to perform.

Putting dots on the spine to identify books is time-consuming, delays weeding until the study is completed, and adds a new function to a circulation center. It is suggested that *all* circulating libraries return to the book card system of circulation control. Under this system, the book cards that have been filled up should be kept in the books and the cards of books that have been removed from the collection should be retained. There has been no evidence that the transaction card or other systems are either faster or better, and many libraries have been destroying one of the most valuable records available for collection maintenance.

This data was not used in the past partly because no one knew *how* to use it. In light of our present knowledge, the simplest way to weed is to return to the book card system, which records each circulation usage (and keeps that record in the shelved books).

However, it is possible that the system of *marking spines* still might be a more efficient system, since it eliminates the need for computing shelf-time periods; it also avoids opening up the books and removing and reading the book cards. If *book cards* are retained, it takes but a few hours to determine a criterion and a cut-point that will identify the core collection. Using dots, this same task takes perhaps a few years and additional clerical tasks. With *neither* available, the most valid criterion for weeding cannot be utilized. A *charging machine*, which would automatically mark the spine of a book, might solve this problem best of all.

One of the most interesting and immediate effects of using the dot system of use-identification, is the help it gives to the acquisition effort. It is a major finding of this study that a high concentration of dotted books in a narrow class indicates a need for more books in this class. It is one of the best indicators for purchasing, if the acquisition policy is to buy books that will satisfy *user demand*.

It is not suggested that this be the only technique to determine candidates for acquisition. In Harrison, after only a few months, a rapid walk around the library showed areas of heavy use and areas of almost no usage. Within classes, travel, gardening, sports, fiction, and picture books were heavily used. Religious books, philosophy, and biography books were over-represented. Purchases in those subjects were reduced. It is not suggested that *all* the books acquired be in the most used classes, only that a real emphasis be placed in those areas.

Closely related to the above is the data uncovered showing that Harrison's library is out of balance, if one assumes a meaningful relationship between use and holdings (see Table 12, page 92).

This is an indication that classes of books are not purchased in relationship to their likelihood of being used. It is the recommendation of this study that, consistent with the desire for a balanced collection, books be bought in areas where they are most likely to be used over a reasonable period of time. The buying patterns that are intuitive or that represent some vague kind of professionalism are not maximizing the financial resources.

There were many seasonal patterns that emerged. In Harrison, when schools and families went into their summer vacations, usage went down, children appeared less often, and assignments were discontinued. Special books with seasonal interest increased in usage. For example, early in the summer, European travel books were heavily used. Later, gardening, golf, and tennis were very popular.

In addition, there were many changing patterns of use that have not been heavily noted in the literature or that perhaps related to this specific community. The circulation of biographies seemed to be falling off. Such changing library trends were easily discerned when red dots were used to indicate circulation.

Books in inaccessible storage had almost no usage. This was the third time that this phenomenon had been noted. For five months, not one single dot appeared on a collection of volumes that had been weeded from the main collection and stored in the basement. This collection was mostly duplicate or older editions of titles held in the main collection. Access to such volumes was by special request and few users even knew of their existence. They might just as well have been discarded.

A technique was suggested for reweeding a core collection of books that already have red dots on their spines. The technique requires that the original procedure be reversed. Each time a volume circulates, the dots are to be *removed* from the spine. Then, when 95 percent of the volumes coming to circulation have no dots on the spine, the unmarked volumes are the core collection and the volumes with dots still remaining are the candidates for weeding. This procedure could be reversed any time an additional weeding was to be undertaken. Inherent in this suggestion, however, is acceptance of the idea that collections be weeded as a whole and not by class. If classes are considered separately, the removal of dots must not start until the last class is weeded.

An alternate approach is being tried at Harrison. Here, blue dots are to be applied to the upper portion of the spine after the first weeding. This is probably simpler than removing dots, although it changes the appearance of the spine considerably. From early computation, it seems as though patterns similar to those developed in the first weeding/study period will redevelop in the next: many books kept in the core collection will now be identified as part of the non-core collection. Weeding seems to be required on a continuing basis.

APPENDIX E

HISTORICAL RECONSTRUCTION METHOD OF CREATING SHELF-TIME

EXPLANATION OF METHOD

Because of the certainty with which Fussler and Simon[1] rejected the "circulation reconstruction method" and insisted that the "historic reconstruction method" was the only valid means of establishing shelf-time periods, the *Five Library Study* compared these two different methods and showed rather clearly that both methods produce the same results, within statistically acceptable ranges. For this reason Fussler and Simon's contention has been rejected.

The Sample. In the Briarcliff Library, the sample consisted of 10 percent of the fiction holdings of the library. Every tenth volume on the shelves and in circulation was inspected. The following pertinent information was recorded for each volume:

1. The number of circulations that occurred in each of the last three years.

2. The last three circulation dates recorded on the book cards in each volume.

3. The loan period for each volume—four weeks, two weeks, or one week.

4. The date of the first recorded circulation.

5. The most recent imprint date.

6. The date of the first circulation, if fewer than three complete years of information existed on the card.

7. The McNaughton Collection holdings.

The Problem. This part of the study attempted to reconstruct three complete years of circulation history as it related to the shelf-time periods and to compare such conclusions with the results uncovered by observing the same variable at circulation for a few days. The results can be seen in Table 35.

Certain serious problems existed in Briarcliff. Only two shelf-time periods per volume were recorded. All other shelf-time periods were estimated. If there were 10 or more uses per year, it was estimated that these uses all fit into the zero shelf-time period (remaining on the shelf thirty days or less). If six to nine uses had occurred, the one-month shelf-time period was assumed. Further shelf-time periods were estimated as shown on page 164.

Table 35

PERCENT OF THE CIRCULATION SATISFIED AS DEVELOPED BY THE
"CURRENT CIRCULATION METHOD" COMPARED TO THE
"HISTORICAL RECONSTRUCTION METHOD," BRIARCLIFF

Shelf-Time Period (Months)	Circulation Sample (Current Circulation Method) All Usage at Circulation for Several Days	Collection Sample (Historical Reconstruction Method) Total Uses in the Last Three Years
0	72%	75%
1	79	87
2	85	91
3	86	93
4	90	94
5	94	95
6	96	-
7	97	96
8	-	-
9	98	97
10	-	-
12	-	98
20	99	99
30	100	99.8
40	-	-
50	-	-
60	-	-
64	-	100

Number of Uses	Shelf-Time Period, in Months
5	2
4	3
3	4
2	6
1	12

It is obvious that these might have been somewhat inaccurate, but on the average they are realistic.

A much more serious problem was that the McNaughton Collection was being returned at the rate of 10 percent per month. It turned out that the average McNaughton book had been in the collection only about four months. Therefore, on the average, many books that had actively circulated during 35 of the 36 reconstructed months had been removed, and no usable information existed, either in their book cards or in any other form.

It was assumed that whatever patterns of use characterized the present collection of McNaughton books also characterized the previous use of this collection. The missing data was supplied by multiplying the current McNaughton Collection data by 9.1, the exact ratio of missing-to-existing data. The missing data thus supplied by estimation represented almost half of the total 6,744 circulations reported for these three years.

As in the rest of this experiment, there was no way to tell what happened with weeded books or with those that had new book cards. It was felt that this lack would not have a practical effect, since the results at the useful end (99 percent of retained future use) would be affected only minimally by well-used books. Furthermore, this library had done very little weeding, except for the McNaughton Collection.

CONCLUSIONS

While more study is needed in this area, and while at least one year of sampling of some sort is called for (to avoid seasonal use patterns that may distort final results), no advantage has been found in the much more arduous and incomplete process of "historical reconstruction" of circulation patterns. From a practical point of view, the current circulation method seems to offer a superior, practical method for creating weeding criteria.

As can be seen in Table 35, at any weeding level above the 94 percent keeping level, the results are within a range of ±1, well within a range caused by normal and expected sampling error.

REFERENCES

1. Herman H. Fussler and Julian L. Simon, *Patterns in the Use of Books in Large Research Libraries* (Chicago: University of Chicago Press, 1969).

GLOSSARY

Better Predictor. The criterion that will yield a core collection of fewer volumes that will still satisfy a given level of future use.

Classic. An older book that exhibits the same circulation pattern of new books.

Closed-End Shelf-Time. The time period between the last two uses of a volume.

Compact Storage. Various methods of storage that will accommodate more books in a given area than will a conventional stack arrangement.

Core Collections. Sub-set of the holdings that can be identified with reasonable assurance as being able to fulfill a certain predetermined percentage of the future demand on the present collection.

Current Circulation Method. The sampling of books as they circulate in order to determine use patterns. This is done by examining books or book cards at the circulation desk to obtain data. It assumes that current patterns of use at circulation are a valid sample of the total use pattern.

Cut-Off Period or Point. The exact time point that determines whether a book is in the core or the non-core collection; i.e., the criterion to be used for weeding.

Cut-Point. Same as "cut-off period or point."

First Shelf-Time Period. Shelf-time period for a book before its first circulation; this can be determined only if the date of shelving is recorded.

Five Library Study. A 1969 research project undertaken by the author in five libraries: Briarcliff and Tarrytown, in New York, and Morristown, Trenton, and Newark, in New Jersey.

Harrison Study. A research project in which the theoretical findings of the *Five Library Study* were put to practical use in weeding the Harrison Public Library.

Historical Reconstruction Method. Ideally, this means reconstructing the entire usage history of each volume in a collection by using circulation dates on *all* book cards since acquisition.

Historical Reconstruction Method, Modified. Reconstructing history of usage over a shorter period of time—in this study, three years.

Imprint Date. Age of a book as indicated by the most recent date printed on the title page or verso.

Keeping Level. The percentage of predicted use to be maintained after weeding.

Level of Future Use. Predicted percentage of use to be retained by the core collection; likelihood of future use of a work, based on its past use.

McNaughton Collection. A collection of pre-processed current volumes rented from the Bro-Dart Company, paid for by a monthly fee, segregated from the rest of the collection. One-tenth of the collection may be returned each month, and new selections received.

Model. Idealized standard for comparison.

Most Efficient Cut-Point. A shelf-time period where the percentage of volumes indicated to be kept is greater than the percentage of future circulation likely to be retained.

Non-Core Collections. Sub-set of the holdings identified as representing a very small amount of the likely future use of a collection.

Open-End Shelf-Time Period. The description of the characteristics of the whole collection; the time that has elapsed between the last use of the book and the date of the study. It measures the most recent length of time in which no use has been made of the volume.

Preferred Method. The most successful method found for developing shelf-time periods to be used as criteria for weeding.

Primary Collection Areas. Open stack areas, accessible to users, which house the regularly used collection.

Secondary Collection Areas. Storage areas less accessible than primary collection areas; normally not open to the user.

Shelf-Time Period. The length of time a book remains on the shelf between circulations. See also "open-end shelf-time period."

Spine Marking. Coded mark on the spine of a volume, which indicates use.

Weeding. Removing the non-core collection from the primary collection area.

Weeding Signal. The first indication that the core collection has been identified, when using the spine-marking method of creating weeding criteria.

Zero Month. A shelf-time cell containing fewer than 31 days.

BIBLIOGRAPHY

American Association of School Librarians and the Department of Audiovisual Instruction of the National Education Association. *Standards for School Media Programs.* Chicago: American Library Association, 1969.

American Library Association. Association of College and Research Libraries. "Guidelines for Establishing Junior College Libraries." *College and Research Libraries* XXIV (November 1963), pp. 501-505.

American Library Association. Association of College and Research Libraries. Committee on Standards. "Standards for College Libraries." *College and Research Libraries* XX (July 1959), pp. 274-80.

American Library Association. Association of Hospital and Institution Libraries. *Standards for Library Services in Health Care Institutions.* Chicago: American Library Association, 1970.

American Library Association. Association of School Librarians. *Standards for School Library Programs.* Chicago: American Library Association, 1960.

American Library Association. Public Libraries Division. Coordinating Committee on Revision of Public Library Standards. *Public Library Service: A Guide to Evaluation with Minimum Standards.* Chicago: American Library Association, 1956.

American Library Association. Public Library Association. Committee on Standards for Work with Young Adults in Public Libraries. *Young Adult Services in the Public Library.* Chicago: American Library Association, 1960.

American Library Association. Public Library Association. Standards Committee and Subcommittees. *Minimum Standards for Public Library Systems, 1966.* Chicago: American Library Association, 1967.

American Library Association. Public Library Association. Subcommittee on Standards for Children's Service. *Standards for Children's Service in Public Libraries.* Chicago: American Library Association, 1964.

American Library Association. Public Library Association. Subcommittee on Standards for Small Libraries. *Interim Standards for Small Public Libraries: Guidelines Toward Achieving the Goals of Public Library Service.* Chicago: American Library Association, 1963.

American Library Association. Small Libraries Project. *Weeding the Small Library Collection.* (Supplement A to Small Libraries Project Pamphlet No. 5.) Chicago: American Library Association, 1962.

American Library Association. Survey and Standards Committee of the American Association of State Libraries. *Standards for Library Functions at the State Level.* Chicago: American Library Association, 1963.

Anderson, Polly G. "First Aids for the Ailing Adult Book Collection," *Bookmark* XXI (November 1961), pp. 47-49.

Ash, Lee. *Yale's Selective Book Retirement Program.* Hamden, Conn.: Archon Books, 1963.

Bedsole, Danny T. "Formulating a Weeding Policy for Books in a Special Library," *Special Libraries* XLIX (May-June 1958), pp. 205-209.

Berelson, Bernard. *The Library's Public.* New York: Columbia University Press, 1949.

Blasingame, Ralph, and others. *The Book Collections in the Public Libraries of the Pottsville Library District: A Date and Subject Distribution Study.* Pottsville, Pa.: Pottsville Free Public Library, 1967.

Boyer, Calvin J., and Nancy L. Eaton. *Book Selection Policies in American Libraries: An Anthology of Policies from College, Public and School Libraries.* Austin, Texas: Armadillo Press, 1971.

Bradford, S. C. "Sources of Information on Specific Subjects," *Engineering* CXXXVII (January 26, 1934), pp. 85-86.

Branscomb, Harvie. *Teaching with Books: A Study of College Libraries.* Chicago: Association of American Colleges and American Library Association, 1940.

Buckland, M. K., and others. *Systems Analysis of a University Library.* Lancaster: University of Lancaster Library Occasional Papers No. 4, 1970.

Busha, Charles H., and Royal Purcell. "A Textural Approach for Promoting Rigorous Research in Librarianship," *Journal of Education for Librarianship* XIV (Summer 1973), pp. 3-15.

Carter, Mary Duncan, and Wallace John Bonk. *Building Library Collections.* 3rd ed. Metuchen, N.J.: Scarecrow Press, 1969.

Cole, P. F. "Journal Usage Versus Age Journal," *Journal of Documentation* XIX (March 1963), pp. 1-11.

Cooper, Marianne. "Criteria for Weeding of Collections," *Library Resources and Technical Services* XII (Summer 1968), pp. 339-51.

Currie, Dorothy H. *How to Organize a Children's Library.* Dobbs Ferry, N.Y.: Oceana Publications, 1965.

Davidson, Carter. "The Future of the College Library," *College and Research Libraries* IV (March 1943), pp. 115-19.

Donahue, Gilbert E. "The Library of the Cowles Commission for Research in Economics," *Illinois Libraries* XXXVII (March 1955), pp. 89-94.

Eliot, Charles William. "The Division of a Library Into Books in Use, and Books Not in Use, with Different Storage Methods for the Two Classes of Books," *Library Journal* XXVII (July 1902), pp. 51-56.

Ellsworth, Ralph E. *The Economics of Book Storage in College and University Libraries.* Washington: Association of Research Libraries, 1969.

Fussler, Herman H., and Julian L. Simon. *Patterns in the Use of Books in Large Research Libraries.* Chicago: University of Chicago Press, 1969.

Galvin, Hoyt, and Barbara Asbury. "Public Library Building in 1973," *Library Journal* XCVIII (December 1, 1973), pp. 3517-23.

Gans, Herbert J. "The Public Library in Perspective," in *The Public Library and the City*, ed. by Ralph W. Conant. Cambridge, Mass.: M.I.T. Press, 1965.

Gosnell, Charles F. "Obsolescence of Books in College Libraries," *College and Research Libraries* V (March 1944), pp. 115-25.

Grieder, Elmer M. "The Effect of Book Storage on Circulation Service," *College and Research Libraries* XI (October 1950), pp. 274-76.

Houser, Lloyd J. *New Jersey Area Libraries: A Pilot Project Toward the Evaluation of the Reference Collection*. New Brunswick, N.J.: New Jersey Library Association, 1968.

Jain, A. K. "Sampling and Short-Period Usage in the Purdue Library," *College and Research Libraries* XXVII (May 1966), pp. 211-18.

Jain, Aridaman K., and others. "A Statistical Study of Book Use Supplemented with a Bibliography of Library Use Studies." Unpublished Ph.D. dissertation, Purdue University, 1967.

Katz, William A. *Introduction to Reference Work, Vol. II: Reference Services*. New York: McGraw-Hill, 1969.

Library Association. Hospital Libraries. *Recommended Standards for Libraries in Hospitals*. London: Library Association, 1965.

Lister, Winston Charles. "Least Cost Decision Rules for the Selection of Library Materials for Compact Storage." Unpublished Ph.D. dissertation, Purdue University, 1967.

McGaw, Howard F. "Policies and Practices in Discarding," *Library Trends* IV (January 1956), pp. 269-82.

Morse, Philip M. *Library Effectiveness: A Systems Approach*. Cambridge, Mass.: M.I.T. Press, 1968.

Mueller, Elizabeth. "Are New Books Read More Than Old Ones?" *Library Quarterly* XXXV (July 1965), pp. 166-72.

Mumford, L. Quincy. "Weeding Practices Vary," *Library Journal* LXXI (June 15, 1946), pp. 895-98.

Neufeld, John. "S-O-B Save Our Books," *RQ* VI (Fall 1966), pp. 25-28.

New York Library Association. Standards Committee and Sub-Committees of the Adult Services Section. *Proposed Standards for Adult Services in Public Libraries in New York State*. New York: Library Association, 1969.

Orne, Jerrold. "Academic Library Building in 1973," *Library Journal* XCVIII (December 1, 1973), pp. 3511-16.

Polson, Ruth E. "When Your Library Joins a System, What Can You Expect?" *Illinois Libraries* XLIX (January 1967), pp. 26-38.

Ranck, Samuel H. "The Problem of the Unused Book," *Library Journal* XXXVI (August 1911), pp. 428-29.

Richards, J. S. "Regional Discards of Public Libraries," *PNLA Quarterly* IX (1944), pp. 15-18.

Rider, Fremont. *Compact Book Storage*. New York: Hadham Press, 1949.

Rider, Fremont. *The Scholar and the Future of the Research Library*. New York: Hadham Press, 1944.

Ruef, Joseph A. "Fertile Fields for Weeding," *Library Journal* LXXXVI (March 15, 1961), p. 1112.

Silver, Edward A. "A Quantitative Appraisal of the M.I.T. Science Library Mezzanine with an Application to the Problem of Limited Shelf Space." Unpublished term paper for M.I.T. graduate course 8:75, Operations Research, 1962.

Slote, Stanley J. "An Approach to Weeding Criteria for Newspaper Libraries," *American Documentation* XIX (April 1968), pp. 168-72.

Slote, Stanley James. "The Predictive Value of Past-Use Patterns of Adult Fiction in Public Libraries for Identifying Core Collections." Unpublished Ph.D. dissertation, Rutgers University, 1970. (University Microfilms, Inc., Ann Arbor, Michigan, No. 71-3104.)

Special Libraries Association. "Objectives and Standards for Special Libraries," *Special Libraries* LV (December 1964), pp. 672-80.

Stieg, Lewis. "A Technique for Evaluating the College Library Book Collection," *Library Quarterly* XIII (January 1943), pp. 34-44.

Stoljarov, Ju. N. "Optimum Size of Public Library Stocks," *UNESCO Bulletin* XXVII (January-February 1973), pp. 22-28, 42.

Trueswell, Richard W. *Analysis of Library User Circulation Requirements.* Amherst: University of Massachusetts, 1968.

Trueswell, Richard W. "Determining the Optimal Number of Volumes for a Library's Core Collection," *Libri* XVI (1966), pp. 49-60.

Trueswell, Richard W. "A Quantitative Measure of User Circulation Requirements and Its Possible Effect on Stack Thinning and Multiple Copy Determination," *American Documentation* XVI (January 1965), pp. 20-25.

Trueswell, Richard William. "User Behavioral Patterns and Requirements and Their Effect on the Possible Applications of Data Processing Computer Techniques in a University Library." Unpublished Ph.D. dissertation, Northwestern University, 1964.

Trueswell, Richard W. "User Circulation Satisfaction vs. Size of Holdings at Three Academic Libraries," *College and Research Libraries* XXX (May 1969), pp. 204-213.

U.S. Department of Health, Education, and Welfare. *Survey of School Library Standards*, by Richard L. Darling. Circular No. 740. OE 15048. Washington, D.C.: Government Printing Office, 1964.

Woods, Donald A. "Weeding the Library Should Be Continuous," *Library Journal* LXXVI (August 1951), pp. 1193-96.

INDEX

173